TOULOUSE-LAUTREC

TOULOUSE-LAUTREC

Gérard Durozoi

CRESCENT BOOKS

NEW YORK/AVENEL, NEW JERSEY

Originally published by Fernand Hazan, Paris 1992

English language edition first published in Great Britain
by Studio Editions Ltd,
Princess House, 50 Eastcastle Street,
London W1N 7AP, England

Copyright © 1992 Fernand Hazan, Paris
English Text Copyright © 1992 Studio Editions Ltd
Translation by Olga Grlic

This 1992 edition published by Crescent Books,
distributed by Outlet Book Company, Inc.,
A Random House Company, 40 Engelhard Avenue,
Avenel, New Jersey 07001

Printed and bound in Hong Kong

ISBN 0 517 06732 3

8 7 6 5 4 3 2 1

INTRODUCTION

Toulouse-Lautrec's fame is ambiguous: too often the painter is overshadowed by the personality. This has encouraged anecdotes to flourish, conjuring up pathos through his famous silhouette, his staccato speech, his shady reputation as a lover of dubious haunts, his long-lasting attachment to Montmartre, legends of which have been retrospectively constructed through his paintings. In view of his self-imposed marginalization, chronic illness, temporary insanity and interrupted work, it is surprising that he has not become an 'accursed' painter. The reason why he has escaped such a description lies in the fact that the initial violence of his canvases has been progressively softened through the generally reassuring myth of the easy women of the Moulin Rouge, where the champagne makes one forget the other, darker side of such a life.

If only he had left a text, a theory explaining his intentions, his conception of painting, but there is nothing, or almost nothing, merely two sentences: 'One paints in the absence of anything better', and 'if my legs had been a bit longer, I would not have painted' – an invitation to interpret painting as nothing more than compensation for his physical deformity.

Following the family tradition – he belonged to a house of rich old Legitimist aristocrats which traced its genealogy all the way back to the Middle Ages – Henri de Toulouse-Lautrec-Montfa would have painted anyway, but as an amateur, just as his father, his grandfather or his uncle had done. Those who enjoyed hunting and hawking also developed a certain taste for the arts: it was all part of the aristocratic *savoir-vivre*. Henri's father, the Count Alphonse, modelled a clay animal from time to time. As an intrepid rider, he was the pride of his lancer regiment before his marriage to his cousin, Adèle Tapié de Céleyran. The marriage did not diminish his passion for the hunt; he gladly travelled from Albi to Sologne for an old-style chase.

A child's education was a job for women: the mother and two grandmothers did enough to spoil their 'Little Pearl' in whose good nature and curiosity they rejoiced. From one residence to another (and the choice was plentiful: the hôtel du Bosc in Albi where Henri was born on 24 November 1864, the château du Bosc in the Aveyron, and the Céleyran castle in the Aude with its 3,700 acres, partially planted with vine) he could be as capricious as he liked. This 'golden childhood' was punctuated by brief visits from an eccentric father who was crazy about dressing up, could perform a 'dance of the savages' in the family drawing room and, on 1 January 1876, dedicated a *Treatise on Ancient and Modern Hawking* to his son. It advises: 'Should you one day experience the bitter side of life, a horse above all, then a dog and a hawk can be precious companions and will help you to forget a little.'

A horse, a dog and a hawk: the formula could seduce the child, who was in the habit of drawing animals, silhouettes and caricatures on the margins of his notebooks, executed with a skilful stroke of the

Young Routy at Céleyran, *c.1883*.
Oil on canvas, 61 × 49 cm
Musée Toulouse-Lautrec, Albi

pencil. Henri was impatient to go riding himself, but was quite sickly. It was doubtless a case of difficult growth, in spite of his outdoor life and good appetite.

In the autumn of 1872 he went to Paris with his parents, who rented an apartment in the Cité du Retiro, and he joined the eighth grade in the Lycée Fontanes – nowadays called the Lycée Condorcet. He met his cousin Louis Pascal again and encountered Maurice Joyant, who was to become his lifelong friend, future publisher and posthumous biographer. Though his father took him to riding school as a means of strengthening him, his health did not improve. He was taken to spa resorts (Amélie les Bains), to the seaside (Nice), and various cures were attempted, but his education had been disrupted, and on 9

January 1875 he left school once and for all, to continue his studies at home, in Albi and in Bosc.

In spite of migraines, painful warts and chronic fatigue in his legs, he remained passionately interested both in horses (in January 1876 he acquired a work illustrated by Crafty, a great specialist in equestrian images) and in drawing, a topic on which his uncle Charles was generous with advice and encouragement. Henri would later acknowledge this debt in a letter reporting his first success to him: 'I hope you will be pleased, for any gleam of sketching ability that I show has been kindled by you . . .'[1] On top of this he was cheerful, even if he often needed to use a cane – something previously unthinkable in the Lautrec family – and found himself 'limping on the left leg'.

On 30 May 1878 in Albi, while attempting to get up from a low chair, Henri broke his left thigh-bone. His foot probably got stuck in a cross-bar of the chair. As his leg needed to be put in plaster, he moved around in a type of small cart. His recovery was very slow: after convalescing at Albi he was taken to Amélie les Bains, Barèges and Nice, where he spent that winter.

A second fall took place during another stay at Barèges, in August 1879. As he had only recently given up the contraption supporting his left leg, he was advised not to walk too much. However, he wanted to join his mother on a walk, and a missed step sent him falling into a ditch barely a metre deep, this time fracturing the right thigh-bone.

Again long months of convalescence were necessary, at the end of which came the terrible final verdict: Henri's legs had stopped growing and he was condemned to remain for ever a deformed 'dwarf'. Some medical experts now think that these health problems may have been due to a rare bone disease, pycnodysostosis, which could appear as a consequence of inbreeding, common in aristocratic families. At the age of thirteen, Lautrec was less than five feet tall, and he was later to gain only one more inch. This was not all: his nose grew progressively broader, his lips swelled, his face assumed an unusual, almost revolting appearance. His 'unpleasant, coarse voice' became more and more nasal and his childhood lisp increased to the point of deforming his pronunciation.

This put an end to Henri's childhood hopes and dreams of riding and hunting. Did he at least have an adolescence? No doubt, but a greatly limited one. He was deprived both of his impulses and of his most secret emotions. Nevertheless, Lautrec did not expect any pity; he was the first to make fun of himself, and his sense of humour – though often black – aroused the admiration of his friends. Forced to toddle with the help of a small cane, his 'boot hook', he was not likely to forget that gracefulness 'was not his gift', nor did it represent 'his salient feature' – but very soon the desire to transcend these physical limitations became apparent.

Wherever he went, he accumulated drawings, watercolours and sketches. Then he began to work in oil: the landscapes of Céleyran follow in a style not unconscious of Impressionism, with their quick little brushstrokes. Nevertheless, he was not as skilled in fixing a silhouette or a posture. He wrote to his friend Etienne Devismes about his landscapes, saying that he was 'completely unable to do them. . . . My trees are like spinach and my sea resembles whatever you want.' In a few months things improved, the trees were no longer like spinach, but they still required more effort to paint than horsemen, harnessing, still life or studies of heads. Lautrec worked hard: the painting was no longer just a pastime, it became more than an escape or a way of proving that, in spite of a weaker body, he could give meaning to his life. In 1880 he produced 300 drawings and about sixty oils.[2] It was still too early to distinguish the beginning of a style within such diverse themes and restrained compositions, but such production generally showed that Lautrec had begun exploring his chosen domain. From then on he devoted himself entirely to the cult of the Holy Palette.

His studies suffered; he failed his baccalaureate examination in July 1881. His mother expected him to retake the exam in August, but instead he illustrated with twenty-three drawings a short story by his friend Devismes, *Cocotte* (a tale about a horse), and sent them to him signed 'a painter who is still green'. After that he resumed 'the dictionaries and the good school book' and received his baccalaureate in Toulouse.

Having thus freed himself, he again took up his palette, brushes and pencils and succeeded, thanks to his uncle Charles, who believed in his growing talent, in joining his parents in Paris in order to pursue a true artistic career. In the capital he again saw René Princeteau, who had already given him some advice. A specialist in hunting and racing pictures with something of a reputation, and a friend of Count Alphonse and uncle Charles, Princeteau had been born deaf, but had later learned to speak, however imperfectly. This disability probably helped to establish a complicity between Lautrec and himself, and made him especially attentive to his 'student's' real progress. He confirmed that it was time for Henri to start a serious apprenticeship: his daring *At the Chantilly Races* (1879), where his sense of movement was displayed, and the *Reminiscence of Auteuil* (1881) contained more than promise. Princeteau did not hesitate to judge a drawing by Lautrec as 'perfect', and his enthusiasm surprised even Count Alphonse himself, as the young would-be painter described in a letter to his uncle: 'Princeteau has been raving. Papa doesn't understand what is happening. We have discussed every possibility – even, just imagine, Carolus Duran. Anyway, here is the plan which I think holds out the best hopes: the Ecole des Beaux-Arts, the Atelier Cabanel and some time at the Atelier René.'[3] A perfect academic programme.

In March 1882, however, Lautrec started working with Bonnat, whilst keeping in touch with 'René's studio', located at 233 rue du Faubourg Saint Honoré, a short distance from the Cité du Retiro, in a building where a number of other 'fashionable' artists worked. One of them, the famous John Lewis-Brown, often accompanied the two friends to the races, the Bois de Boulogne and the Cirque Fernando.

With firm intentions of acquiring all the necessary technical skills, Lautrec joined the studio of Bonnat, to whom he had been recommended by Henri Rachou, a young painter from Albi who was already the 'master's' pupil (page 51). Léon Joseph Florentin Bonnat, born in 1833 and a member of the Institute since the previous year, was one of the best-known (and most expensive) portrait painters and a collector of old masters. His apparent ambition was to imitate their style as anonymously as possible. Certain critics reproached him with painting 'the great shining geniuses who came to him daily with demands to immortalize them on his canvases without spontaneity and with cold photographic precision',[4] but more often he was considered a 'painter of energy and will'.[5] He did not have a reputation for being soft with his students, who had no chance of being tempted by the latest theories (especially Impressionist); and Lautrec, who had a preference for lighter shades, was ordered to darken his palette. In May 1882 he reported on his master's judgement: 'Your painting is not bad, it is stylish – but, in the end, that's no bad thing; on the other hand, your drawing is simply atrocious.'[6] Nevertheless, he complied with the discipline, copied the plaster casts, made his drawing more banal – but was ready to restore all of its vitality as soon as the vacations had begun.

In September 1882 Bonnat, who became professor at the Ecole des Beaux-Arts, closed his studio and let all of his students go. Lautrec probably did not have time to learn a great deal from him, but in going there (to the impasse Hélène, near the place Clichy) he discovered Montmartre and its population, so different from the people he knew in the Cité du Retiro. Since he needed a new teacher he followed some of his colleagues to Cormon's studio, which was located in the rue de Constance and then later at 104 boulevard de Clichy. In a letter to his father he described

Cormon as 'the young and already well-known painter of the famous *Cain Fleeing with his Family*, which is now in the Luxembourg Museum. A powerful talent, austere and original'. Cormon was about to become the academic specialist in prehistoric subjects, but he was also a dreamer, enjoying jokes in the studio: his students nicknamed him 'Father Knee-cap' because of his skinniness. Like Bonnat, he was probably hostile to Impressionism, but he encouraged his students to work 'out of the studio' as much as possible. In the beginning, Lautrec complained about his relaxed attitude: his corrections were 'more benevolent than Bonnat's', but if we are to believe his friend Gauzi's *Memoirs*, the master and pupil got along very well: 'Cormon laughed at his cracks while giving his, mainly benevolent, opinion about the drawings.' On the other hand, Lautrec showed remarkable assiduity; he would arrive at the studio in the morning and would work with models in the afternoon, either at Rachou's or in another garden in the rue Forest. He studied the nude, executed a few allegorical compositions and worked even harder because sometimes he felt lost: 'I am in a pitiful mood . . .' During the summer in Céleyran he was still encountering the same difficulties in painting landscapes; he found 'spots like spinach, pistachio, olives or excrement on my painting'.[7] His desire to learn led him to visit the Louvre and the Salons, where his father had taken him while he was still a child. He began by admiring Detaille, Puvis de Chavannes and Roll but later definitely preferred Degas and Forain.

Among Cormon's pupils, he made long-standing friendships with a number of young artists who were full of new ideas, such as Emile Bernard (see page 57), Louis Anquetin (1861–1932) and René Grenier. The last already led an independent existence, unlike Lautrec himself, who returned home every evening to his mother. Lautrec appreciated Anquetin's landscapes painted 'in an Impressionist style', and they travelled together on several occasions. Of all his friends from this period, Emile Bernard was the most interested in modern artistic ideas. He was involved in

Count Alphonse de Toulouse-Lautrec
driving his mail-coach, *1880.*
Oil on canvas, 38.5 × 51 cm
Musée du Petit Palais, Paris

avant-garde radicalism and was responsible for the introduction of contemporary theories of colour to Cormon's studio. Lautrec, who shared a studio with René Grenier, combined Cormon's academic treatment with the new experimental styles introduced by his more adventurous fellow students. This caused no tension with the master, since Cormon actively encouraged his students to work outside his atelier. At that time Lautrec also started engaging in technical experiments. He would attach 'a sheet of tracing paper to his charcoal study and paint over it'. Such use of tracing emphasized the contours and simplified and stylized the effect he achieved. It also enabled him to dissociate the charcoal drawing from the colour, which was applied directly with a brush – and so his drawing became colour. Degas had achieved the same effect by using pastel, but Lautrec was the only artist to use this tracing technique and he may well have invented it.

He was liked by his friends and spent a lot of time with fellow students from Cormon's atelier. René Grenier and his wife Lily entertained a great deal and enjoyed fancy dress parties. 'After lunch everyone would dress up and group themselves in costumed tableaux. Then they would take great delight in photographing these masquerades ... Lautrec, with the aid of articles from Lily's wardrobe, became in turn a robber, a Japanese man, a choir-boy, or a Spanish dancer', reported François Gauzi. This is how another friend, Henri Rachou, remembered him from that period: 'His most striking characteristics, it seemed to me, were his outstanding intelligence and his constant alertness, his abundant good will towards his friends and his profound understanding of his fellow men.' His repartee was appreciated and so were his sense of humour, his high spirits, his elliptical language, and his use of the word 'Tech-nique', to which he seemed to extend a strange, almost universal meaning. When, as a studious pupil, he painted some scenes from Merovingian times, he used the academic limitations in an ironical way. In 1894 he parodied in large format (172 × 380 cm) Puvis de Chavannes' *Sacred Grove*, which had then only recently been displayed at the Salon. To the conventional procession of the Muses he added a group of mustachioed artists in top hats with the artist himself in the front row, recognizable by his size and his habitual bowler hat, turning his back to the public.

In December 1883 Lautrec rented a studio in the rue Lepic in order to be more comfortable. This was the first separation from his family and probably was not easy for him: his mother, who held the purse strings, showed more than a little distrust of the artistic milieu ('studio life, excellent from the point of view of work, is otherwise a hard test for a young man') and thought of Montmartre as a 'bad neighbourhood'. 'An art student up to his neck', he wore a beard just like the rest of his colleagues and 'worked like a horse', but was not so sure of what he should do. Anquetin's advice was to join him 'in the Impressionist way', but Lautrec already knew that it was not his style. His

Photograph of Lautrec dressed as a choir boy, with Anquetin and Grenier, 1880.

paintings dealt more and more with the human figure.

He spent the summer of 1884 in Paris, instead of going to the south-west and, as he decided against taking the entrance exam for the Ecole des Beaux-Arts, Cormon asked him to collaborate on illustrating the complete works of Victor Hugo. This was a great boost for the young painter, since he was the only one from the studio who was invited to work on the project – even though his drawings for *La Légende des siècles* were not used in the end. The requirements of this project provided the excuse to move in with his friends René and Lily Grenier, at 19 bis rue Fontaine – the same building in which Degas had his studio. This time, the break with the family was complete: aside from a simple change of residence, the style of his painting changed. His mother and probably also his father had envisaged a fashionable career for him, something like Bonnat's, respectful of convention and rewarded by admission to the Institute. Lautrec's discoveries led him in a completely different direction, however.

In the 1880s, Montmartre certainly did not correspond to the image we have of it today – itself created by Lautrec – but the neighbourhood was different from the rest of Paris. Its almost village-like appearance, its mixed population of artists, 'easy' women, artisans and petty crooks, with whom fashionable society was soon to come into contact, its balls and bars set it apart from the rest of the town.

When the young artist moved into the neighbourhood there were still vineyards and large gardens all around, but numerous artists already worked in the area. Its main artery, the boulevard de Clichy, was also the imaginary boundary which separated the studios of established artists, such as Puvis de Chavannes or Degas, in the south, from the cheaper accommodation in the north favoured by younger and less well-known painters. The entertainment industry of Montmartre, its *cafés-concerts*, cabarets and dance halls, concentrated mainly around boulevards Clichy and Rochechouart and, at first, frequented by the local working-class population, soon began to attract a public drawn from the Parisian middle classes. The entrepreneurs quickly understood the commercial potential of Montmartre and its flourishing entertainment industry, and the number of new establishments increased rapidly.

Lautrec frequently visited its places of entertainment, where his appearance was not at all shocking. As he walked over to Cormon's studio, or visited his friends (Rachou lived in the rue Ganneron at the bottom of the Montmartre cemetery), he could not ignore the silhouettes, behaviour or attitudes of the passers-by. The streets were busy with shop assistants, washerwomen, little seamstresses or prostitutes, but also longshoremen, bourgeois traders and fleeting figures of people engaged in illegitimate business. Such a population, completely overlooked in the painting of the period because it did not conform to the values and ideals which such an art aimed to represent, interested only the 'illustrators' like Willette or Steinlen. Nevertheless, this obverse of normal society, or at least its margins, presented itself as a new world – which needed to be seen in a sharper way, transposed

on paper or canvas without predetermined meanings being imposed on it.

While the production of drawings did not slow down, the small number of oils painted in 1884 (around ten) indicates the hesitations and difficulties Lautrec encountered in looking for what he needed to find. There were no sudden breaks with tradition in his painting style, but a gradual transition which is traceable through his works of the period. The *Cart Stuck in the Mud*, a *Sous-bois* ('Undergrowth') and a *Horseman Following a Stag Hunt* were the final versions of already well-worn themes. The *Bust of a Man* and the *Flute Player* remain academic exercises, but two female nudes indicate the turning-point which Lautrec was about to reach. If *Jeanne* (Rijksmuseum Kröller-Müller, Otterloo) still belonged to a conventional setting (the seated model turned three-quarters, with lowered eyes and anaemic-looking flesh), the *Fat Maria, the Venus of Montmartre* (Von der Heydt Museum, Wuppertal), in spite of the awkwardness of the drawing and the mediocrity of the play of light, reveals a readiness to expose reality without disguising it. The prostitute faces the viewer's gaze frontally, and has a scornful or defiant expression on her face, as if the posture of this compliant and available body was able to tear through the veins and varnish with which the painting (the gaze) protected itself from reality.

In November 1884 Lautrec wrote to his mother: 'I am back in the old routine that will last until spring, and then maybe I'll do some really bizarre things. All vague yet.'[8] Two months later he was still hesitating about 'preparing something for the Salon'. 'All this is quite ambitious and requires reflection.'[9] This reflection was to be cut short: the fascination with Montmartre overcame the Salon.

The Montmartre which he frequented was less that of the Butte than the Boulevard. In fact, Lautrec was to become a regular figure in the numerous cabarets and brasseries rapidly multiplying all along the boulevard de Clichy and the boulevard de Rochechouart: Le Rat Mort, La Boule Noire (renamed La Cigale after 1887), the Café des Colonnes, the Elysée Montmartre and Le Chat Noir, which was opened in 1881 by Rodolphe Salis. The reputation of the last establishment was founded on its owner's glibness of tongue – a mixture of fake obsequiousness and daring – and the luck of attracting to its décor of odds and ends, crowned with a painting by Willette, a regular public composed of artists and writers. It is not clear whether Lautrec cared for his personality very much, but Le Chat Noir was where Aristide Bruant, who was going to play quite a different role from Salis in Lautrec's life, had his début. When he bought the establishment in 1885, Bruant renamed it Le Mirliton and he soon became famous, as much for his repertoire of 'pitiful verse' and 'vindictive refrains' full of carefully worked slang as for the hospitality he proffered to an ever greater clientele. If we are to believe the reports, 'he welcomed the army, toasted with the Académie, abused cads, exposed imbeciles, upbraided the powerful, referred to grand dukes as regular cossacks and was disrespectful to royalty.' This is how Rodolphe Darzens described the singer in 1889, at a time when he was already widely known: 'As for Aristide Bruant, everyone knows him. Tall, with a broad barrel chest and a Napoleonic profile; but his eye is sly and his lip sardonic. He wears sweeping velvet garments, heavy boots and, when he goes out, a long Inverness cape and an immensely wide-brimmed hat.' This is the figure we shall find on several of Lautrec's posters (page 85).

A true friendship, which endured for many years, soon united the two men and their collaboration was to enhance the fame of both of them. Thanks to Bruant, Lautrec began to pick up the atmosphere of Montmartre: the contempt for established values, the mixing of social classes and the contact with a reality beyond the reach of official art. He still continued to work with Cormon and entertained his studio by loudly singing Bruant's refrains. The singer could be reproached for an excessive populism, but that was the best means of attracting attention to the most hidden and secret aspects of society. 'Bourgeois? We eat them alive at the Mirli!' exclaimed Paul Roinard, one of the regular visitors to the cabaret.

Although the atmosphere of the cabaret had changed with his ownership, Bruant did nothing to change its décor – except for suspending from the ceiling the Louis-Treize chair left behind by his predecessor Salis. This mascot became the subject of one of his songs, which in turn inspired Lautrec for two of his paintings, *The Song of the Louis-Treize Chair* and *The Quadrille of the Louis-Treize Chair at the Elysée Montmartre*. Besides providing inspiration for Lautrec through his songs, Bruant displayed the young artist's paintings in his cabaret and asked him to provide illustrations for his songs for publication in *Le Mirliton*, the magazine which he issued at irregular intervals.

Bruant's *Le Mirliton* was not the only publication linked to a particular cabaret. Le Chat Noir had its own eponymous magazine and *Le Courier français* was affiliated to the Elysée Montmartre. Other more ambitious periodical publications, such as the *Paris illustré* and *Figaro illustré* (connected to the Boussod et Valadon gallery in Montmartre), featured illustrated articles about the Montmartre arts scene, gossip about cabaret stars and information on the latest performances and other attractions. To these magazines Lautrec regularly submitted drawings, many of which were first published in their pages before being sold separately in the Paris auction houses, at times even without the artist's authorization.

Bruant, for one, guessed that Lautrec belonged to a different realm from Willette or Steinlen (who nevertheless illustrated his collection *Dans la rue*), and it is possible that his own style influenced the painter's new development. Little by little, in 1885, Lautrec gave up studio models and became interested in the people around him (as shown by the portraits of Lily Grenier and Emile Bernard), but also in the women he

*Photograph of the cabaret
entertainer, Artistide Bruant*

not long before said that he could render 'the accuracy of the body's life under the life of fabric'. Like Degas, he still portrayed proper ballerinas, in tights and tutus.

In 1886 *The Quadrille of the Louis-Treize Chair at the Elysée Montmartre* substituted for classical choreography gestures which belong to a different genre, where graceful movements are replaced by the splits, dancing on points by high kicks and the ethereal image of the female body by an aggressive exhibitionism. The *Quadrille* in grisaille was displayed for a long time in the cabaret and was used by Lautrec as the basis for a cover illustration for the December 1886 issue of *Le Mirliton*. It represents characters invoked to symbolize the frenzy of Montmartre night life: 'Father Decency', who supervised the dancers so that they would not go too far in exposing their flesh, and especially La Goulue ('The Glutton') and Grille d'Egoût ('Drain Cover'), who were to become famous thanks less to their talents as dancers than to Lautrec.

In spite of its modest size (45 × 56 cm) this *Quadrille* has a symbolic value; hanging as it did in Bruant's cabaret in the heart of Montmartre at its most exuberant, it shows to what extent Lautrec had become attached to the neighbourhood and how his gaze was attracted by its most typical spectacles.

Whether he lived with the Greniers, with his friend Doctor Bourges in the rue Fontaine or worked at Cormon's or Rachou's, he was always at the foot of the Butte. Starting in 1886, he rented a bigger studio in the building where Gauzi and Steinlen also worked, at 7 rue Tourlaque, a street in which numerous studios were occupied by artists who, unlike academic painters, could appreciate the advantages of natural light coming in through the large bay windows. Four years later Renoir was to move into a studio in the same street and Lautrec stayed until 1897. While some of the neighbours periodically suffered poverty, his comfortable financial circumstances, due to the

passed in the street, such as the worker Carmen Gaudin (page 53), to whom he devoted four portraits. While we can still discern in these paintings certain aspects which refer to the teachings of Cormon or Bonnat, they also attest to the artist's fascination with Degas. He was indebted to Degas's dancers and when, during the winter, he spent a few days in Villiers sur Morin and undertook the decoration of the inn, Le Régisseur, the works he executed on the walls – the *Dancer in her Loge*, the *Ballet Scene* and the *Poulterer* – amply illustrate this debt. His efforts generally grasp the true movement, the right attitude, as far removed as possible from any conventional form – just like Degas, of whom Octave Mirbeau had

Detail from Hangover, *c.1887–8.*
Black and blue crayon, brush and black ink on paper,
49.3 × 63.2 cm
Musée Toulouse-Lautrec, Albi

family vineyards, did not stop Lautrec from turning his studio into a curiosity shop full of a mixture of furniture, worthless objects, drawings pinned on the walls and piles of canvases. A box concealed his collection of Japanese knicknacks, for which he had developed a taste in Bonnat's studio when the American paintor Harry Humphrey Moore had shown him what he had brought back from his latest voyage in the Orient. The parody of Puvis de Chavannes presided over all of this.

Suzanne Valadon also lived at 7 rue Tourlaque. After a number of odd jobs she had had to interrupt her acrobatic career as a result of a fall and had started modelling, notably for Puvis de Chavannes, but also for Renoir and Degas. Finally, encouraged by the Italian painter Federico Zandomeneghi, who was known as Zando, she had begun to paint. Lautrec's relationship with her encouraged his visits to Le Chat Noir, Le Mirliton and the Elysée Montmartre even more, but the affair ended painfully: she made fun of him, which only confirmed the poor opinion he held – or pretended to hold – of women. He had had his first sexual experience with a semi-prostitute, which had not filled him with enthusiasm. Ever since his cousin Jeanne d'Armagnac had looked after him following his fall ('She is so tall and so beautiful . . . I am neither tall nor handsome'), he had learned to hide his tenderness, to play the cynic ('That one, I could have her whenever I want – for 50 francs') and to take advantage of services provided for paying clients by specialized parlours. When, in merry company, he exclaimed: 'Oh, the life, the life!' should we read into this an expression of joy or suffering? Most likely, its meaning changed moment by moment: whatever Lautrec thought about life was revealed in his paintings.

Work did not slow down as Lautrec began to define his own style. The only things he borrowed from the Impressionists were their brushstrokes and a taste for light shades and natural lighting. He was not at all interested in their theories about creating shapes with rays of light; when he placed his models out of doors, the natural setting was not elaborated, but served only as a background against which the figure – the only thing which interested him – was outlined.[10] From that point of view, his two portraits of Suzanne Valadon (1885) were exemplary; they inaugurated a series of female portraits continued until 1891, which turned Lautrec into a first-rate portrait painter, precisely because he captured the psychological presence of the model more than her relationship to the background. Regardless of social position, the face, but also the posture, the expression, the curving shoulder, the sloping back, all began to symbolize an intimate truth which the painting had set out to reveal. Contrary to the academic portraits which

continued to proliferate, Lautrec did nothing to normalize the human figure, to make it conform to the socio-aesthetic categories to which the Salon public was accustomed. He banished allegorical props and artificial poses; he broke with the pictorial rhetoric which codified the propriety of paintings by subordinating representation to pre-existing intentions. Whereas portrait painters all over Europe (Bonnat, Alfred Stevens, Jacques Emile Blanche, Ilya Repin, Charles Giron or Paul Chabas)[11] often featured standing models – if only better to expose the clothing or surrounding furnishings – and posed them in such a way that they dominated the spectator, Lautrec readily composed figures cut off at the waist or halfway down the legs, inverting the relative position of the viewer. He did not care to exalt a social image and allowed himself every freedom to concentrate on what he perceived as truth, even beyond immediate physical appearance. In the portrait now in the Ny Carlsberg Glyptotek, Copenhagen, Valadon is shown with a face which does not correspond to her actual age: Lautrec adumbrated what she would look like fifteen or twenty years later.

This readiness to go beyond both the visible data and the conventional (or convenient) representation of things and beings is more apparent in the series consisting of four studies and an unfinished painting entitled simply *Artilleryman and a Woman* (Musée Toulouse-Lautrec, Albi). Whereas the influence of his oldest teacher and friend René Princeteau is still visible here, we can also observe the development of Lautrec's fluid technique in which oil paint was treated like watercolour. Aside from showing how Lautrec composed his characters by working on successive drafts (and he was to remain faithful to this method, especially in preparing his posters), we can also point out the nervousness of the drawing, and above all the crudeness of the idea: the scene represents nothing more elevated than a soldier getting dressed in front of a prostitute. There are no embellishments: if that is how things happened, that is how the painting had to represent them, without superfluous ornamentation or prudery.

As he pursued this direction, Lautrec became more and more indifferent to the specialist debates which excited his colleagues. They could not count on him to spend whole evenings discussing theoretical questions. If anyone attempted to draw him in, he would respond firmly: 'Don't bother me with that!' He had better things to do with his evenings: the tours of the bars, cabarets and brothels became longer and he was often able to lure his companions along as well.

Enjoying farce more than pontificating discourses, in 1886 he participated in the Fifth Exhibition of Incoherent Art, a group founded in 1882 by an old member of the 'Hydropathes' (the so-called 'Water-haters'), Jules Lévy, who always made the news in the sort of press publications read by Lautrec, such as *Le Chat Noir*, *Le Courrier français* and *Le Gil Blas*. Hiding behind the pseudonym Tolav-Segroeg ('A Hungarian from Montmartre who has visited Cairo and is staying with a friend, he has talent and has proved it', according to the catalogue), he exhibited an 'oil painting on emery-paper': *The Batignolles, Three and a Half Years Before Christ*.[12] His love of jokes led him to dress up at the first opportunity, whether at costume balls or parties with friends: we can see him as a choirboy, a clown, a second-class cabaret singer, adorned with a feathered boa and a matching hat, a kimono, and so on. His sense of humour was nevertheless different from that of his contemporaries; while he appreciated, for example, Willette's drawings in *Le Courrier français*, he claimed that he was unable to find captions to accompany his own croquis, which resemble realistic sketches more than cartoons. He could not treat reality like an artist such as Steinlen, but distinguished himself from contemporary illustrators, particularly through his rejection of all sentimentality: in Lautrec's drawings there is no sympathy, complacency or scorn – instead we find a penetrating gaze, and certainly not a moralizing point of view. When he was

Artilleryman and Woman, c.1886.
Oil on tracing paper, 56 × 45 cm
Musée Toulouse-Lautrec, Albi

making fun, it was usually of his own physical appearance and he did it with the utmost cruelty: much more than contemporary portraits by his friends (Maurin, Rachou, Vuillard or Bonnard), his self-caricatures underline the deformity of his features, his short legs and his spiky beard. And when he put himself in his paintings – often with his back turned, or as an extra in the crowd – he would readily put a very tall person next to himself (his cousin Gabriel Tapié de Céleyran, beginning in 1891), creating a clown-like couple which he then exhibited in the bars and theatres. In this way, he anticipated any predictable mockery, becoming himself the master of all derision.

In order to rest from the life he led in Montmartre, starting in 1885 he regularly spent his summers in the château de Malromé, which his mother had bought two years previously. He would often go there by sea, from Le Havre (most often aboard the *Chili*, on which he gained his reputation as a cook by treating the crew to his American-style lobsters), and then from

Bordeaux, where he had access to the brothel in the rue de Pessac. After reaching his mother's house, he would go on to the Bassin d'Arcachon. In Taussat he had a small boat, the *Cocorico*, and would enjoy the physical exercises in which he excelled: sailing, swimming, and fishing with cormorants (we could be forgiven for seeing this as a parody of his father's fondness for hawking). He surprised his friends with his skill in swimming and diving, which contrasted so dramatically with his cropped figure and awkward walk. Having thus recuperated his forces, upon his return he was more able to take advantage of Parisian pleasures – the Cirque Fernando, the Elysée Montmartre, masked balls at the Moulin de la Galette. In the calm of his studio or père Forest's garden he would rediscover his favourite models (Lily Grenier and Carmen Gaudin, whose red hair obviously captivated him), work on portraits and accumulate drawings from the life.

In 1887 Lautrec began to thin his oil paint with turpentine so that, upon drying, it impregnated the paper or cardboard and acquired a mat or pastel look. Diluted in this way, this *peinture à l'essence* did not slow down the brushstroke and was appropriate for his nervous drawing style. He also began relying more and more on cardboard rather than the more conventional canvas base. His preference for this cheap industrial material as an alternative to the more bourgeois medium was a conscious choice, and cardboard was better suited to his low-life subject matter. At the same time he developed the habit of not painting all of the background, leaving some of it in its original tone, most often the brown cardboard. Why bother with finishing the background? It was just a convention designed to neutralize the principal scene by its setting. It seemed better, in order to suggest movement, merely to outline the silhouettes and postures, leaving the brushstrokes which defined them clearly visible. In this way the dancers – and this was the period in which La Goulue and Valentin Le Désossé ('The Boneless'), the stars of the Moulin de la Galette, began to recur in Lautrec's paintings – could

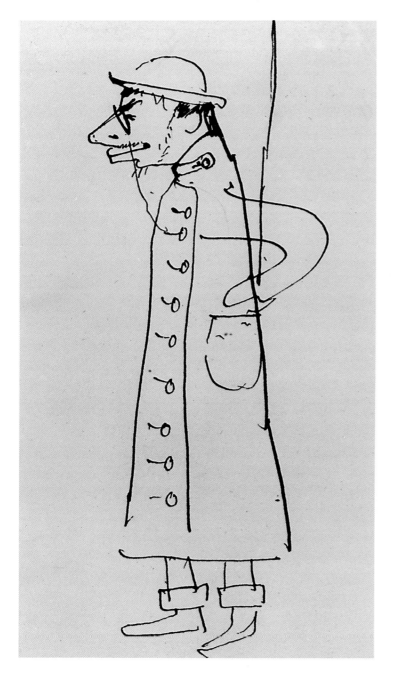

Self-Caricature, c.1885.
Pen and ink drawing
Musée Toulouse-Lautrec, Albi

be represented in all their dynamic movement.

This technique was one amongst many at this period. It was most likely that Lautrec first met van Gogh, who was part of Cormon's studio, in the autumn of 1886. The two young painters liked each other; they went out to the same haunts and van Gogh often brought a recent canvas to the rue Tourlaque, expecting a helpful judgement. As drinking and joking were the primary concerns, he would leave with the painting under his arm, after an hour or two, without having had a chance to say anything. Suzanne Valadon drew the conclusion that 'the painters were stupid', but Lautrec must have been more interested than he showed. This may be seen from the portrait of Vincent, completed in 1887, where he obviously borrowed van Gogh's characteristic crossed strokes and the general colouring (blue, green, orange-yellow). The sitter was shown in profile, leaning against a coffee table, his gaze fixed on a distant point, divided between an object or spectacle outside our field of vision and the interior vision that was already within himself. In the same year, the *Portrait of the Countess Adèle de Toulouse-Lautrec in the Drawing Room at Malromé* (page 59) proved that the debate with Impressionism was far from being closed. How could it ever be when Lautrec visited Renoir so often, when Pissarro lived in the rue de l'Abreuvoir, and when Signac's studio was in the boulevard de Clichy? Was it not the Impressionists who were the first to paint Montmartre and to prove that it was possible to break with academicism?

Lautrec's production was relatively erratic: about fifteen oils in 1887, thirty-five in 1888, twenty-four in 1889, but only eighteen in 1890. Nevertheless, his thematic and stylistic choices became confirmed and

Vincent van Gogh, 1887.
Pastel on cardboard, 54 × 45 cm
Foundation Vincent van Gogh
Vincent van Gogh Museum, Amsterdam

major canvases began to appear, each of them bringing an additional dimension to his work: *At the Cirque Fernando: The Ringmaster* (page 71), *The Laundress* (1889), *The Ball at the Moulin de la Galette* (Art Institute of Chicago), *Pierreuse* ('The Street Walker', 1889, Ford Collection), *Dance at the Moulin Rouge* (page 75). In each painting, the particular motif has been transcended, removed as far as possible from its initial anecdotal or documentary origin, in order to reach a certain timeless universality. Lautrec presented, above all, a collection of archetypal characters and situations, but he achieved this exemplary generality by evoking particular beings and equally specific locations. Thus, for example, we can identify the man in the bowler hat leaning on his elbow at the right-hand side of *The Ball at the Moulin de la Galette*: it is the painter Joseph Albert. We quickly realize, however, that the model was of no intrinsic importance: what mattered was that the meaning of the dance itself had changed so much since Renoir had painted it in 1876. The delightful summer open-air party and its festive and youthful atmosphere were replaced by a closed space, an atmosphere heavy with gloom and a pervasive, though unadmitted boredom. In contrast to Renoir's characters, radiant young men and women who danced, flirted and chatted with complicity, Lautrec's seem isolated in their absolute solitude. They occupy the indoor hall of the Moulin de la Galette on a late winter night. The cold and alienated atmosphere of the dance hall, populated by seedy-looking men and weary women, is stressed by its sickly colouring and thin, streaky paint. 'Oh, the life, the life!' – its seamy side was decidedly lugubrious, even in the places where one was supposed to have fun.

On 5 October 1889 Montmartre was bustling with excitement; pedestrians and vehicles rushed towards number 90 on the boulevard de Clichy. It was the opening night of the Moulin Rouge which, as well as offering a huge dance hall with a large gallery, boasted a terraced garden with different attractions, such as donkey rides, an open-air *café-concert*, next to which stood an enormous elephant (from the Exposition Universelle), transformed into a small theatre where the entertainment was provided by belly-dancers and the Pétomane. The owner, Charles Zidler, had a clear vision; his establishment was an immediate success and within a few weeks the Moulin Rouge had become a compulsory stop for every night-owl. One could get lost in the bustle, look for an amorous adventure, get drunk on liquor or noise and, above all, take pleasure in watching the dancers performing the *chahut*, also known as the *quadrille naturaliste* (when danced by two pairs of partners). This wilder and more energetic version of the *can-can* consisted of two main movements for the female dancer, based on high kicks and the splits. The dancers were professionals, experienced in exciting the curiosity of the clients by revealing their enticing undergarments, which consisted of layers of petti-coats and lacy knickers. Zidler and his partner Joseph Oller soon hung *At the Cirque Fernando: The Ring-master* (page 71) in the lobby, and Lautrec had his own table reserved in the establishment. Nevertheless, it was at first a poster by Chéret that was used to advertise its attractions, because in 1889 his playful feminine silhouettes seemed to be the most appropri-ate to symbolize the *joie de vivre* of the moment.

For posterity, Lautrec and the Moulin Rouge are undeniably related. The turning-point came in 1891, when Zidler commissioned the artist to design a poster for his establishment. The new image of Mont-martre created by Lautrec through his posters and large-scale paintings played down its sleazy and dangerous side (gangs of thieves still controlled entire streets and scared tourists and potential bourgeois visitors away) to stress instead the glamour of the quadrille dancers. This collusion between the cabaret owners and the artists they commissioned to design publicity that would dispel the fears of their potential middle-class clientele was ultimately beneficial for all concerned. The ever greater competition in the enter-tainment industry stimulated the need for posters, which had proved to be an important advertising technique, and, in turn, this growing demand opened a whole new field for artists and illustrators. The publicity campaigns were obviously successful. By the late 1890s the Moulin Rouge had become a showcase for visitors and was particularly popular among large numbers of English tourists.

In the years up to 1896, Lautrec was to devote some thirty paintings, as well as lithographs and numerous drawings, to the bustling atmosphere of the Moulin Rouge, its performers and its regular clients. Amongst these we find once again La Goulue and Valentin le Désossé, already portrayed in 1887 in the Moulin de la Galette. From that moment on they acquired a central role as a pair of dancers who were particularly remarkable for the number of different roles – as contrasting as their characters – which they assumed. La Goulue, born in 1870 as Louise Weber, had earned her nickname through her appetite and her taste for strong liquor and was, according to Yvette Guilbert, 'pretty and coarsely funny to watch'; on the scene, her suggestive and abrupt movements were full of aggres-sive vulgarity, criticized by some, but also the key to her success. By her side, Valentin (whose real name was Jules Renaudin and who danced for free, spend-ing his days working for his brother, a notary), with his slim and elongated figure, stood in contrast to his well-rounded partner. This phlegmatic man, always wearing his old and battered top hat and smoking the butt of an evil-smelling cigar, led an ordinary exist-ence, unlike La Goulue, who was always involved in amorous adventures with numerous men and women.

Between 1890 and 1892 the Moulin Rouge became the central point in Lautrec's life and work: he found his models among the dancers or the public. Having always complained about professional models and their false poses, he finally had to deal with strong personalities, able to show their interior truth. He used to spend his evenings there, often in the company of his cousin Gabriel, sketching the faces of the revellers and the postures of the dancers, so that he could re-work them later in his studio or on the

Photograph of the Moulin Rouge in Montmartre, with posters by Lautrec

lithographic stone. Above all, he owed his sudden notoriety to the poster commissioned by Zidler to add to the publicity for his dance hall in 1891. So closely did Lautrec become associated in the public's mind with the Moulin Rouge and its greatest star, that a journalist writing in *Le Figaro Illustré* could soon describe the artist as 'La Goulue's official painter' – not exactly what Count Alphonse and his wife had had in mind when they hoped that Henri would become a celebrated society portraitist.

Though he had already completed more than half of his painted output at this date, Lautrec was not yet particularly well known. The public could have heard of him only through the drawings he had published in the press (*Le Mirliton* was followed by the *Paris illustré* and *Le Courrier français*) and through the lithographs, which did not sell very well. Among his friends there were several art lovers who appreciated his work. In 1888 he received a visit from two members of the group Les XX who invited him to exhibit his work in Brussels, where he showed eleven paintings and was recognized by some critics as equalling Seurat, even though James Ensor did not like his work. This was the first exhibition of real significance for him since it marked his official entry into avant-garde circles.

Subsequently Lautrec exhibited a great deal, believing it to be the best way of presenting his work to the public. It was important to him to define himself as a serious artist and participation at prestigious exhibitions was perceived as the barrier which separated the amateur from professional artists. Furthermore, there was no better way to measure oneself against one's professional peers. As early as 1883 or 1884 Lautrec had submitted a portrait of his friend Gustave Dennery to the Salon but 'was refused by 38 votes to 2'. In 1887 he made another attempt, this time with provocative intentions in mind. Using a pseudonym, he submitted a still life representing a Camembert cheese completed with 'a black frame edged with gold'. He was nevertheless furious to learn that his painting had been rejected by the jury. This was not the first time that Lautrec took recourse to a pseudonym in order to protect his family name. His earliest known alias was Monfa, a slight alteration of one of his names. Later he used the simple anagram Treclau for an exhibition in Toulouse in 1887. In the catalogue of the Incohérents' exhibition, all of the artists' names were parodied and for this occasion Lautrec chose the extravagant-sounding Tolav-Segroeg, the 'Hungarian from Montmartre'.

From 1889 onwards he appeared regularly with the Indépendants, and in January 1890 he exhibited again with Les XX. He went to Brussels for the opening of the show, where he challenged Henry de Groux to a duel because the Belgian painter had insulted van Gogh by accusing him of being 'ignorant and full of hot air'. The duel was called off after de Groux retracted his statement. Later the same year, in March, he had two paintings at the sixth exhibition of the Indépendants. He wrote to his mother: 'What a day! But what a success. The Salon has received a slap from which it might recover, but which will make many people think. The Sociéte des Artistes Indépen-

dants was created in 1884 in response to the exclusive policies of the official Paris Salon and the harshness of its jury. The biggest names in Neo-Impressionism exhibited with the Indépendants and Lautrec joined them on many occasions.

He also featured at the exhibitions of the fashionable Cercle littéraire et artistique of the rue Volney, where he reappeared four times between 1889 and 1892, before being 'eliminated' by the jury: 'I did not know that, having paid part of the rent, they had, or they claimed the right to throw out the artists', he wrote angrily to his mother.[13] In 1891 he showed eight works at the seventh Salon des Indépendants. Among them were portraits of his friends Henri Bourges and Gaston Bonnefoy, his cousin Louis Pascal and the photographer Paul Sescau. The novelist and critic Octave Mirbeau remarked upon Lautrec's 'spiritual and tragic strength in his portrayal of faces and his interpretation of character'. These portraits were executed in pigment thinned with turpentine, which underlined his rapid brushstrokes. The same year he exhibited the *Ball at the Moulin de la Galette* once again at the Salon du Palais des Arts libéraux, and in December could proudly write to his mother: 'We have opened a shop, a sort of permanent exhibition in the rue Le Peletier.[14] The papers have been very kind to your offspring. I am enclosing a passage written with honey dipped in incense.'[15] The exhibition, where Bernard and Anquetin showed their works alongside Bonnard and Maurice Denis, had indeed a certain success and the *Echo de Paris* published some of the participants' declarations. Lautrec's was, as always, very laconic: 'I just get on with my work.'

Since they both worked in the same neighbourhood, this devotion to his painting did not stop him from

Study for The Moulin Rouge – La Goulue, *1891.*
Charcoal, stump, pastel, wash and oil on stained paper,
154 × 118 cm
Musée Toulouse-Lautrec, Albi

seeing his old school friend Maurice Joyant almost every day. For the past year Joyant had been in charge of the Boussod et Valadon gallery: the new owners of the premises (they had previously belonged to the Goupil gallery) had asked Joyant to get rid of the 'horrors' accumulated by Théo van Gogh – canvases by Gauguin, Monet, Pissarro, Degas and others . . . and, possibly, some of Lautrec's. Though close friendship with a connoisseur such as Joyant encouraged Lautrec, it did not yet bring him fame.

Photographic portrait of Lautrec with his walking-stick, c.1892.

This came with the poster for the Moulin Rouge (page 79) which assured his glory as soon as it appeared in Paris in October 1891. The poster confirmed the encouraging words which Degas had addressed to Lautrec the previous month, when he had said that his work that summer 'was not too bad'. Work on the poster offered a novel experience to the painter, who was used to solitary work: 'It is indeed very entertaining to do. I had authority over the whole workshop, a new feeling for me.' He worked with the printing workshop Ancourt, where Bonnard introduced him and where he spent, according to Thadée Natanson, 'so many of the happiest hours of his life'.

The success of this first poster brought in new commissions: in a few years, from *The Hanged Man* (page 87) to *La Gitane*, Lautrec revolutionized the art of the wall-poster. Jane Avril and Bruant himself (pages 101 and 85) owed part of their fame to him, but Claudieux, May Belfort and May Milton who, without those images, would have been forgotten – just like the titles of Victor Joze's novels – all owed him even more. Simplification of the backgrounds, frequent use of pure unmodulated colour, and daring and unorthodox layouts were the essential techniques which contrasted with Chéret's pleasant compositions, the effectiveness of which was reduced by unnecessary embellishments. Lautrec realized early in his career that a poster is viewed quickly and that all its elements had to converge in order to reinforce its power to communicate. The editor of *La Dépêche de Toulouse*, Arthur Huc, better known under his pen-name 'Homodei', was fascinated by this process in Lautrec's treatment of Bruant: 'When he created the magnificent poster for Bruant, which is and remains the masterpiece of the genre, he first painted him in detail, as Bonnat might have done. Then, to his sitter's utter astonishment and dismay, he deleted and deleted again, retaining only the essential lines. The basic idea remained sincere. Lautrec's capacity for synthesis had reduced it to an epigram.'

These radical techniques offended the tastes of many

May Belfort, *1895.*
Lithograph poster, 78.8 × 60 cm
Victoria and Albert Museum, London

critics and H. Bouchot, the librarian at the Cabinet des estampes of the Bibliothèque nationale, deplored Lautrec's adoption of 'rudimentary polychromatic sensations',[16] but other specialists quickly understood the full importance of his contribution: 'His technique is the proof of his incontestable mastery . . . In his drawing there is nothing unnecessary or unjustified, and all that is indispensable is there.'[17] Through his thirty-one posters Lautrec made obsolete the production of Chéret, Willette or Steinlen (the last was to pay him homage), who could now only be appreciated for their overloaded and old-fashioned style as museum pieces.[18] The fact that a good number of his creations were not commissions in the narrow sense, but rather

presents he offered to his friends, probably gave him a degree of creative freedom which professional 'advertisers' seldom enjoy. Nevertheless, Lautrec made his mark unconditionally as the true creator of the 'modern' poster. Poster collectors of the period, who quickly started acquiring his sheets, were not proved wrong. Already in 1893 the *Moulin Rouge* was marked as 'rare' and cost 20 francs (in 1896 Bonnard's *France Champagne* reached the price of only 5 francs) and until 1900 Lautrec was well represented at international poster exhibitions.[19]

He was perfectly aware of the innovations which he had introduced in the field, and would hang posters next to his paintings in some exhibitions: at the 'Cercle des XX' in 1892, when his contribution was marked by a flattering article by Verhaeren; then again in 1894 at the 'Libre Esthétique', which replaced the 'Cercle des XX'; and two years later at Joyant's gallery. Thanks to such support he could reach a public made up of all social groups, rather than merely the usual art lovers; if Lautrec did not worry too much about 'democratizing' the art himself, he was certainly not indifferent to wider fame.

He could not hope to conquer the public with his painting, or at least not immediately, particularly as it was at least partially devoted to 'shocking' themes. Portraits of men were acceptable, especially since they most often represented friends, such as Doctor Bourges, M. Lemerle, the poet Georges-Henri Manuel, the photographer Paul Sescau or the musician Desiré Dihau (page 81). On the other hand, female portraits were less easy to place: even though Degas had made a small dent in the established tastes of the period, it is hard to imagine a bourgeois sitting-room – since that was the 'normal' place for a painting – decorated with *The Streetwalker* (page 77) or *The Woman Curling Her Hair* (1891, Musée des Augustins, Toulouse). The scenes of cruel realism (*A la Mie,* 1891, The Museum of Fine Art, Boston, whose title – an allusion to *un miché à la mie,* the slang expression for the client who dodges paying the prostitute –

indicates the nature of the relationship between the characters) or the numerous scenes from the Moulin de la Galette and the Moulin Rouge, which were neither entertaining nor 'decorative', did nothing to make his work more acceptable. Furthermore, Lautrec began producing compositions whose models obviously came from the world in which he became more and more interested: the licensed brothels, known as the *maisons closes*. In 1892, at the request of its 'Madam', he decorated the 'house' in the rue d'Amboise, creating sixteen panels topped by medallion portraits of the residents, the whole project matching the 'Louis XV' style décor of the premises.

Without necessarily wishing to do so, Lautrec distanced himself from official art and its pictorial norms, as well as from the contemporary avant-garde styles. Just as the Impressionist canvases began to seduce educated art lovers with the importance they accorded to nature and light, Lautrec painted only what he saw: the world of artifice and spectacle, of calculated and seductive poses. He avoided the beauty of nature and preferred the more ambiguous charms of nights devoted to pleasure-seeking; he was not attracted by innocence, but by the full self-awareness of a look or a gesture, by the individual's conscious self-representation. For, if it was the painter who defined the point of view, it was the sitters who decided which part of themselves they wanted to show. In his respect for his models, Lautrec's work differed from the habits of contemporary official painting which, under the pretext of exalting them, masked individuals behind their function or social status. For example, the manner in which he treated such a medical celebrity at Dr Jules Emile Péan, in two oil paintings on cardboard from 1891, is significant: in one case (*A Tracheotomy Operation*, originally known simply as *Dr Péan Operating*, Sterling and Francine Clark Art Institute, Williamstown) he was interested as much in the surgeon's professional gesture as in his physiognomy, and in *An Operation by Dr Péan at the International Hospital* (Baumgarten Collection), the great doctor was represented from the

back, so that the looks of his assistants would converge on his dark and – if we were to ignore the title of the work – anonymous silhouette.

Four years later, the leading Academic painter Henri Gervex painted his own version of *Dr Péan Operating in the Hospital Saint Louis* (Musée de l'Assistance publique, Paris); it was a large-scale painting (242 × 188 cm, whereas Lautrec's largest cartoon measured only 74 × 50 cm), celebrating at the same time both medical and artistic techniques. Thus the canvas became a documentary colour print in which, under the pretext of objectivity, surgical instruments, textures and costumes were catalogued and the characters transformed into motionless dummies. Lautrec created tension, Gervex merely designed a display. The former's work was dry and pointed to the essential (the gestures, the looks), the latter drowned his subject in a eulogy of Science. Such an emphasis was more to the taste of the public than the coldness of a Lautrec, who was nevertheless so much more concerned with surgery, as he found that it resembled his own activity: revealing and cutting into living flesh. Some sources indicate that in his youth Péan wanted to become a painter; conversely, Lautrec had been heard to say, 'If I were not a painter, I would like to be a doctor.'

Lautrec met Dr Péan through his cousin Gabriel Tapié de Céleyran, who arrived in Paris from Lille in 1891 to complete his medical studies, soon became the assistant of the famous surgeon and continued working with him until Péan's death in 1898. In a report on Lautrec and his interest in medicine published in a medical journal in 1922, Tapié de Céleyran described the impact the famous surgeon made on the artist,

---

Dr Péan Operating, *1891–2.*
Peinture à l'essence on cardboard, 73.9 × 49.9 cm
Sterling and Francine Clark Art Institute,
Williamstown, Massachusetts

who had always been fascinated by 'all that squirms . . . [Lautrec] lost little time in following me to the Hôpital Saint Louis, where he was soon captivated by Péan's virtuosity. He went every Saturday morning and filled up albums with notes and sketches.' Lautrec's friend Jules Renard also testified to the way the painter was attracted to Péan, 'who can rummage through an abdomen with the air of a man feeling in his pocket for small change . . . and who, slicing like a butcher, discourses urbanely to the lookers-on'.

Already in 1891 Jane Avril appeared in the background of a composition in which La Goulue, with her usual defiant air, dominated the foreground.[20] During 1892–3 she became Lautrec's favourite model, progressively overshadowing La Goulue. Known also as 'The Melinite' (the name of an explosive similar to dynamite) or 'Crazy Jane' (because of her residence in Charcot's mental hospital at the Salpêtrière), she was of greater interest to the painter. With her decadent but sophisticated manner, she provided a dramatic contrast to the superficial exuberance of a 'good girl' lacking a secret emotional life, exemplified by La Goulue. More refined and cultivated, after a tumultuous past which would have been considered banal in her own milieu (as an illegitimate child of an Italian aristocrat and an alcoholic *demi-mondaine*, a prostitute, a runaway and so on), she began to dance in the *quadrille* at the Moulin Rouge, but without any great success. As soon as she danced alone, however, she attracted attention, inventing a new, personal choreography, combined with pantomime, with which she triumphed at the Divan Japonais. To such an enigmatic personality all kinds of vices and different perversions have been attributed, but her seductiveness had its basis as much in the calculated harmony of her stylish outfits as in the energy which lurked within her.

She was unusually cultivated for the circles in which she moved, and was acquainted with several well-known contemporary poets and artists. Her friendship with Lautrec was complete: she played the hostess when he received guests in his studio; he took her out to the best restaurants and gladly spent whole days in her company; he would go to fetch her in a carriage when she posed for him and, above all, she really appreciated his painting. He represented her on a cover for *L'Estampe originale*, he represented her in the process of examining a print in Ancourt's workshop: a well-deserved homage to her good judgement. The importance which Lautrec accorded to Jane signalled a change in his habits: he began to lose interest in dances and broadened his acquaintance with *cafés-concerts* and, later, with the theatres, continuing all the while to work on his portraits of prostitutes and brothel scenes.

In cabarets and theatres he found a high level of professionalism and a milieu where the silhouette, the gesture and the glance were loaded with meaning. Their best performers knew how to conceal the amount of practice that went into perfecting their gestures and postures in order to achieve a superior verisimilitude which revealed the psychology of life itself. On the stage the value of preparation or synthesis came to the fore, whereas in the brothels the women fascinated Lautrec outside their work, while they were resting after their clients had left and they relaxed, forgetting themselves, occupied only with the needs of their own bodies. On the one hand the utmost artifice, and on the other the display of the natural; but in both cases Lautrec tried to capture the truth which others were not yet able to see.

When his friend Doctor Bourges got married in 1893, Lautrec could no longer live with him and did not know where to turn. He did not enjoy living alone and complained in his letters about the prospect of running his own household: 'I shall have the ineffable pleasure of keeping my own household accounts and knowing the exact price of butter.' He started eating with his mother, who lived in the rue de Douai, but did not easily adapt to his new solitude and started to spend more and more time in large, established brothels. He became the confidant of the residents,

A woman lying in bed, c.1896.
Pencil and wash on laid paper, 29.2 × 47.5 cm
Courtauld Institute Galleries, London

brought them presents, shared their intimacy, took part in their moments of relaxation. On Sundays they sometimes 'drew lots' for him: his sexual prowess had long ago earned him the significant nickname of 'The Coffee-Pot'. Above all, Lautrec observed the fleeting moments: he captured the kisses and the tender caresses between two friends; he drew sleeping bodies, unconscious abandonment, tea-table gossip, card-games, the toilette; he accumulated drafts, sketches and quickly executed drawings which, in his studio in the rue Tourlaque, he later used for portraits, some nudes and group scenes. However, with the exception of the three versions of the *Staircase of the rue des Moulins*, in which a woman was figured provocatively crawling up the stairs, he never used them for 'erotic' or licentious compositions.

Lautrec was neither a voyeur nor a moralist;[21] he represented these women as they revealed themselves once they had given up the tawdry finery and the obligatory smiles required by their profession – their bodies, attitudes and faces in which were perceptible fatigue and boredom, weariness or a slight remnant of youthful hopes, the marks of time, and, secretly, the gloomy side of an existence in which moments of true pleasure were so rare. The idea recurring throughout the fifty or so paintings which he had devoted to the them, starting in 1893 and until the peak of *The Salon on the rue des Moulins* (pages 107 and 109), is that in such places more could be found than the death-like tremor of the orgasm: Eros and Thanatos were closely linked, as a certain Dr Freud and his followers had discovered in Vienna. But in Paris, Lautrec revealed this secret through his painting technique, as is suggested in his *Femmes de Maison* ('Prostitutes'), with their flabby flesh, swollen faces, rare smiles fixed like the grin of death, and the cheeks under which one can almost make out the bones.

At the same time as Jane Avril, another vedette of the Parisian scene began to fascinate Lautrec more and more. In the 1892 poster for the Divan Japonais (page 101) we can perceive only her elongated silhouette without the head, but in July 1893 two drawings reproduced in the *Figaro illustré* confirmed her identity: it was Yvette Guilbert. After a difficult start as a dressmaker, a mannequin, and later several fruitless débuts in the theatre, an experience from which she learned her perfect diction (thereby reversing the usual trend for the stars of the day), she turned to the *café-concert.* She reached the peak of her popularity in the following year, having worked at the Eden Concert, the Moulin Rouge and the Divan Japonais. Unusually tall and slim, she cultivated her shortcomings in order to stress her personality and, wrapped in green satin dresses with a plunging neckline, she sported her long black gloves as a distinctive sign. She described the reasons of her particular style in her memoirs, published in 1927: 'I was looking for an impression of extreme simplicity, which allied itself harmoniously with the lines of my slim body and my small head . . . I wanted, above all, to appear highly distinguished, so that I could risk anything, in a repertoire that I had decided could be a ribald one: mingled with veiled satire, but still direct. To assemble an exhibition of humorous sketches in song, depicting all the indecencies, all the excesses, all the vices of my 'contemporaries', and to enable them to laugh at themselves . . . that was to be my innovation, my big idea.' Lautrec listened to her singing, produced many drawings of her silhouette, her features, her

Yvette Guilbert singing 'Linger, Longer Loo', *1894.*
Peinture à l'essence on cardboard, 57 × 42 cm
Pushkin State Museum of Fine Arts, Moscow

gloves, her crossed fingers; he analysed her attitudes, the gestures with which she bowed to the public while holding on to the curtain, and so on. He wanted to do a poster for her, but the singer, who inspired many different talents of the period (Capiello, Sem, Léandre, Bac, Camara), had already commissioned one from Steinlen. While waiting for an appropriate occasion, Lautrec, with his friend the chronicler and celebrated art critic Gustave Geffroy, devoted an illustrated album to her. One hundred copies of this album were produced and signed by the singer. It had an immediate success. In *La Vie Parisienne* a critic wrote: 'Yvette Guilbert. Her glory is complete! She has now been described, depicted, analysed in a volume that will be a delight to all bibliophiles with a taste for the extraordinary. For such is the decree of that subtlest and acutest of critics, Gustave Geffroy; and the most audacious draughtsman, Toulouse Lautrec, has captured her in her many poses. This apotheosis of the *diva* of the *café-concert* is something quite out of the ordinary. It is a book that will endure, because it is unique of its kind.'

The singer herself appreciated Lautrec's work: 'Thank you for your beautiful drawings in Geffroy's book. I am very pleased! So pleased! And you have all my gratitude, believe me.' So she wrote to him, though she was nevertheless reticent towards the painter's proposals because she found that he went too far in what she called – in a significant slip – 'his genius for distortion'.[22] The poster was never executed, but in the minds of lovers of the French *chanson* and its historians, the silhouette of Yvette Guilbert will for ever be that which was captured by Lautrec in his rejected project (page 111).

It was the same thing with his image of Loïe Fuller, an American from Illinois, who gave up a successful career in opera and vaudeville and devoted herself entirely to the dance (page 105). Her routines, in which she twirled veils attached to wands that she held in her hands, were enhanced by creative lighting provided by a team of specialist stage electricians under her brother's direction, using various devices such as mirrors and strobe effects. Lautrec was not the only contemporary artist, by far, to be captivated by her spectacular play with veils, but he was nevertheless the one who left the most dynamic and synthetic vision of her. Such too was the fate of the clowness Cha-U-Kao, whose real name, concealed behind a Japanese-style stage-name based upon a wordplay on the title of a popular dance, we do not even know today. She possibly never reached the highest levels of public acclaim, but was limited to comic interludes between the main attractions. None

the less, with the four portraits which he painted in 1895 (page 115), Lautrec conferred upon her an almost mythical dimension and made her an equal of the big contemporary stars. Her impassive features, her conical hairdo, and her clown-like collar were enough to conjure up the intermixture of the music-hall and the circus, while at the same time they represented, for the painter, a sort of good-bye to the sawdust. Other spectacles, other milieux were already calling him.

In the company of the writer Romain Coolus, Lautrec went more and more often to the theatre. His artistic production in the period between 1891 and 1898 concentrated chiefly on the personalities associated with theatrical life, as the portraits of Lucien Guitry and Jeanné Granier, and the drawings of Sarah Bernhardt, Monet-Sully and Réjane show. He designed programmes for the Théâtre Libre and made lithographs inspired by it (*The Large Theatre Box, Programme for 'L'Argent'*). He would return several evenings in a row to the same show, tirelessly sketching in order to capture a pose, making several portraits of the actress Marcelle Lender. In 1894 he finished his *Dr Tapié de Céleyran in the Theatre Corridor* (page 113): his faithful evening companion was now placed in a different décor from his customary setting of the Moulin Rouge. Lautrec was not just a spectator, he also collaborated in theatrical productions. Thus, in December 1894, he worked with Louis Valtat on the scenery for *The Little Clay Cart*, a classical Indian play adapted by Victor Barrucand for the actor Lugné-Poé:[23] from this project a model of the exotic landscape and the massive silhouette of an elephant have survived. We also have the programme cover: standing on the elephant, there is a draped figure with outstretched arms; this was the figure of the critic Félix Fénéon.

Although we do not know to what extent, it seems that Lautrec also participated in the creation of *King Ubu* in 1896, together with Bonnard, Vuillard and Sérusier. Without being one of his closest friends,

Alfred Jarry was one of the writers with whom Lautrec was acquainted. Writing a review of the Salon des Indépendants two years previously, the writer had stressed the presence of 'a beautiful Toulouse-Lautrec', and in *King Ubu's Almanac* of 1899, listing 'important people who are in the news', he 'epically' described the painter as 'the poster man'.[24]

The names of Coolus, Jarry, Lugné-Poé and Fénéon conjure up the 'friendly and always welcoming *Revue Blanche*' which had been founded in Belgium by Paul Leclercq in 1889 and then published by the Natanson brothers sinces its transferral to Paris in 1891. Its last issue was published in 1903. Succeeding Thadée Natanson, Félix Fénéon became its editor-in-chief in January 1895, having lost his job at the War Ministry after a trial during which he was accused of having been in possession of bombs. Already in 1889 he had noticed Lautrec's work at the Salon des Indépendants (*The Ball at the Moulin de la Galette*) and later praised his merits as a poster designer in the anarchist journal *Le Père Peinard*.[25] He discovered that Lautrec had been socializing with the members of the *Revue Blanche* since 1894. The magazine was the meeting-point of all that counted in the literary and artistic worlds of Paris. The young André Gide, his friend Paul Valéry, Tristan Bernard and Alfred Jarry, creator of the infamous 'King Ubu', were amongst the regular contributors and the review also published prints by avant-garde artists such as Bonnard, Vuillard, Denis, Roussel, Sérusier, Cottet and Redon. As Thadée Natanson testified: 'What Lautrec liked in that milieu was that it was so exceptional ... At the *Revue Blanche* they talked about painting and works of art in a way which pleased him. Lautrec enjoyed the kind of French they used, which was often spicy, but always beyond reproach. But nothing pleased him more than hearing Renoir or Rodin praised, if it was not to talk about them with companions whom he made almost as appreciative as himself of a roast leg of lamb, cooked for seven hours, or a bottle of Entre Deux Mers, which he would bring for lunch with exaggerated care.' In this milieu of writers and artists,

Lautrec really felt at home. Like the rest of them, he was seduced by the beauty of Misia, Thadée's wife, and he used her silhouette for a poster in 1895 (page 116). She charmed him with her interpretations of Debussy and Fauré on the paino and this is how he represented her in the portrait which he completed in 1897. The Natanson circle provided the theme for a great number of drawings, lithographs and paintings and, at the request of the youngest of the brothers, who also wrote for the *Revue Blanche* under the name of Alfred Athis, he conceived his last poster in 1899 for Jean Richepin's play *La Gitane*, in which Alfred's wife, the actress Marthe Mellot, played a leading role.

The Nathansons entertained a great deal, both in Paris and at their country villa La Grangette in Valvins, where Lautrec occasionally went to enjoy the outdoor life and his favourite sports, rowing and sailing.[26] Through them he became friends with Romain Coolus, Jules Renard and Tristan Bernard, met Maurice Donnay, Octave Mirbeau and Léon Blum, and saw Bonnard and Vuillard once again. In spite of his continuing taste for night life and brothels, Lautrec did not neglect these social connections: he felt appreciated at his true merit; to be one of 'the artists of the *Revue Blanche*' meant to be a member of a circle in which the most daring artistic experiments were conducted with an inimitable blend of seriousness and good humour. In the *Revue* itself, aside from some vignettes and a portrait of Oscar Wilde sketched during an encounter in London in 1895 (drawn from memory, since the great Irish writer, raconteur and wit declined to grace Lautrec with a sitting), he was represented mainly by the caricatured and aggressive illustrations which he made for the Supplements – as, for example, in the July 1894 issue – of *Le Chasseur de chevelures*. He also published his parodies, often touching on the obscene, of the canvases exhibited at the Salon des Champs Elysées, and in the first issue of the *Nib* he accompanied Tristan Bernard's texts with his lithographic sketches, one of which represented a circus scene that showed the clown Footit giving his partner Chocolat a kick in the bottom.

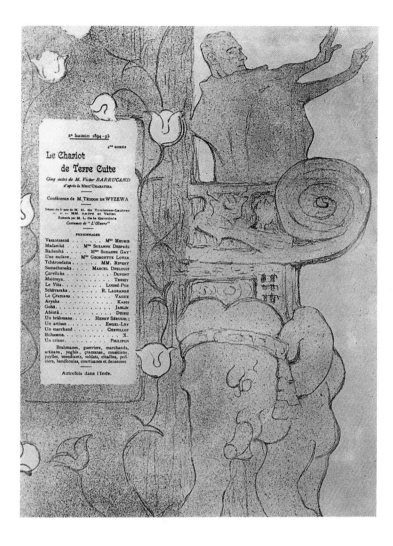

Programme for The Little Clay Cart, *1895.*
Chalk lithograph with spatter, 43.8 × 27.8 cm
Bibliothèque Nationale, Paris

It was also thanks to the *Revue Blanche* that Lautrec had the unique opportunity, during a party organized by Alexandre Natanson to unveil his new dining-room panels which had been decorated by Vuillard, of demonstrating his mastery in the art of cocktail making. That evening, disguised as an impeccable barman, with his head entirely shaved, he poured 'more than two thousand glasses' to three hundred guests – from Fénéon to Bonnard, Mirbeau, Rebell, Boylesve, Vuillard and Pierre Louÿs – and got them intoxicated to such a point that many did not survive until the end of the reception. Lautrec himself, how-

ever – exceptionally for him – did not touch a drop of alcohol all evening.

His connections with the *Revue Blanche* were symptomatic of his status in 1894–5; although he was not well known to the general public (he was, after all, only thirty), Lautrec was on his way to becoming an eminent member of artistic circles. After his exhibition at Boussod-Valadon in 1893, he had won the support of some art critics (especially Gustave Geffroy and Roger Marx, but also Ernest Maindron, who published an article about him in *La Plume* in November 1895, and L. Muhlfeld, who wrote about him in the *Revue Blanche*). He collaborated on journals such as *Le Rire*, whose editor-in-chief Arsène Alexandre was a good friend, and he contributed to *Pan* in Germany. Always in touch with the new tendencies in architecture and the decorative arts, he brought from Brussels (where he had met Henry Van de Velde) a collection of Art Nouveau carpets and pottery. More and more often he had the opportunity of showing his own work in satisfactory surroundings, at Samuel Bing's, for example, whose gallery opened in 1895 and where the exhibitors' canvases were hung next to Art Nouveau objects and Japanese prints. Lautrec stepped up the production of lithographs, which included menu cards as well as original compositions.

Nevertheless, these activities, and his relative integration into the contemporary artistic milieu, were not enough to guarantee Lautrec his mental stability. His taste for drinking became more and more pronounced and an ever greater cause for worry to his relations. It was not unusual, after a night of drinking, to see a carriage stationed in the small hours in front of the lithographic workshop: Lautrec would have a few moments of rest in it before resuming work. If his physical resistance was remarkable, his mental state was volatile: successively, he had outbursts of violent anger, would sink into a strange lethargy or burst out laughing for no particular reason – 'When drunk,' noticed Thadée Natanson, 'he choked with laughter.'

His alcoholism became more and more mundane; it fluctuated according to the places he went to, but was getting progressively worse. Abandoning Montmartre little by little, with the exception of La Souris, a bar close to the Place Pigalle whose lesbian patrons tolerated his curiosity, he moved to the neighbourhood of the Opéra, to the 'English' or 'American' bars where he enjoyed the company of cab drivers, actors and circus artistes. He appreciated the wood and leather décor of these bars, their ambience which was at one and the same time 'chic' and cosy, and the variety of drinks they offered. He continued to work intensely on his drawings, and sketched, among other things, both Chéri-Bouboule, the bulldog belonging to the owner of La Souris, and Footit dancing. Above all, though, he drank, swallowing anything indiscriminately, from the foulest drinks to the most expensive and exquisite ones, until he would reach the required level of intoxication. In his letters to his mother, which had stopped talking about painting long ago, he periodically expressed worries about his wine stock and his income – he was spending a lot.

In 1896 he held two one-man exhibitions at Joyant's gallery. The first, in January, consisted of paintings and drawings, and the second, in April, presented his most recent lithographs. Lautrec himself invited the Naturalist novelist Edmond de Goncourt, who was not at all impressed with what he saw and later, in an entry in his diary, described Lautrec as 'a ridiculous little man whose caricatural deformity is reflected in every one of his drawings'.

That summer he went with a friend to Taussat, via Le Havre, Bordeaux and Malromé. They almost continued the boat trip all the way to Dakar because of an unknown woman who fascinated Lautrec (*The*

Reine de Joie, *1892.*
Lithograph poster with brush and spatter,
149.5 × 99 cm
Private Collection

Passenger in Cabin 54, which later served as a poster for The Salon des Cent). In the end, his travelling companion, Maurice Guibert, managed to persuade him to disembark in Lisbon. They visited the museums of Toledo and Madrid and spent the rest of the summer in Taussat.

At this time, his pictorial production began to suffer; he produced some thirty compositions in 1896, but only about twenty in each of the following three years. Nevertheless, among the portraits and the genre scenes, there were still several masterpieces – for example, at the end of 1895, *The Sofa* (Museum of Modern Art, New York), on which two prostitutes in long black stockings lie in abandoned rest, or *Marcelle Lender dancing in 'Chilpéric'* (1896), which represented the peak of his series of works on the theatre. This last large-scale canvas (145 × 150 cm) was the final outcome of a long fascination with the actress, a fascination apparent in the large number of drawings and lithographs he made of her, in the way he constantly attended her performances, but also in his behaviour which the object of his interest found disturbing – as when, for example, the painter would sit opposite her in a restaurant and focus his penetrating gaze on her, analysing her physiognomy without uttering a single word. *Chilpéric* was an operetta parodying Merovingian times in which Queen Galeswinthe – of Spanish origin – danced a bolero. In this musical number Lautrec found everything he looked for both in a woman and in a theatrical performance: grace, elegance, extreme forms of artifice, and perfect mastery of the body, which became a spectacle in itself. His canvas, with its crude colours, its 'preFauvism' and its composition in which, around the central swirl of the actress, grotesque extras were arranged in a half-circle, did not please Marcelle Lender and the artist gave it to his friend Paul Leclercq. This work was at once a symbol of his love for the theatre and a turning-point in his painting technique: the layers of colour were more thickly applied, the drawing style less allusive – it seemed as if Lautrec was implicitly challenging the fundamental

Marcelle Lender, *1895.*
Bust-length lithograph portrait
in six colours, 32.5 × 24.6 cm
Victoria and Albert Museum, London

Chilpéric there were other successes: the portraits of *M. de Lauradour* (Private collection, New York) and *Paul Leclercq* (page 129), *The Toilette: Madame Poupoule* (1898, Musée Toulouse-Lautrec, Albi), *The Englishwoman of the 'Star' in Le Havre* (page 131) and the 'miracle' of *The Milliner* (page 137). Nevertheless, most of the oil paintings produced in these three or four years were frequently different versions of previous compositions, or reprises of some of the themes abandoned long ago, particularly horses and riding scenes. The only new motif which appeared at this stage was bicycling, as in *Tristan Bernard at the Buffalo Bicycle Track* (1895). This theme did not appear in his painting again, however, but was developed in two posters (*Bicycles Michäel* and *Simpson's Lever Chain*, 1896).[27] This slowing down in the production of paintings was not followed by a more generalized diminution in the output of graphic works. On the contrary, menu cards, posters, lithographs and illustrations flowed in a constant rhythm, as if Lautrec were finding, in the field of graphics, more and more satisfaction, and a swiftness and facility of production which were no longer evident whenever he took up his brushes. It was also noticeable that some of his oils were intended as studies for lithographs; if this was not a novel procedure, it did become more frequent at this time and the lithographs seem to have attracted more of his interest than painting – perhaps due to their easy distribution.

From 1896 onwards, Lautrec's existence was governed by well-established habits: the bars, the prostitutes, the friends, a little painting and the summers he spent at Taussat to recover a healthy and care-free appearance. There he dressed up as a muezzin and scandalized the neighbours as much by swimming in the nude as by the scenes with which he decorated the fence that was supposed to protect the nudist's privacy. A few vacations in the countryside during the rest of the year, especially with the Natansons, and a few trips abroad (Toledo and Madrid in 1896, the Netherlands in 1897, and London in 1898, where he exhibited seventy-eight works, but without much

tenets of academic painting, showing what they all ought to have done with their technique. Having approached their themes and their compositions in this way, Lautrec also brushed against their ideology: could one 'save' the beauty of Marcelle Lender in a grotesque context which threatened to degrade her? In order to respect the painter's intention, when we examine this painting we ought to separate the admiring look directed at the actress from the critical one directed at her surroundings, whereas the uniform pictorial treatment invites an undifferentiated gaze.

After the portrait of Marcelle Lender dancing in

success) broke a possibly monotonous routine. Occasional sales reassured and flattered the painter: the exiled king of Serbia, Milan Obrenovich, acquired *At the Moulin Rouge* and *The Clowness Cha-U-Kao*, and Isaac de Camondo, the famous collector, bought another portrait of the clowness and added it to his collection of paintings by Monet, Manet and Degas (it was hung in a bathroom – although with a Manet, which should have been a consolation). On top of everything else, his insatiable curiosity, his hunger to observe the world around him, made him return tirelessly to the theatres and lesbian bars to collect an ever increasing number of visual impressions.

In 1897 Lautrec installed himself in his new atelier in 15 avenue Frochot[28] and summoned all his acquaintances to celebrate the event: on the small lithograph which he sent out in the guise of an invitation, he represented himself as an animal tamer getting ready to milk a cow – the invitation was for a 'cup of milk'. There was no need to worry, however, as a good selection of cocktails was also prepared. The new studio was closer to his mother's apartment in the rue de Douai, where he was still eating regularly. This 'saintly woman and mother', as he portrayed her, or 'the old lady with beautiful hands who went to mass every day', according to Paul Leclercq, never stopped worrying about her son's health and the people with whom he socialized. The new studio was also closer than the rue Tourlaque to La Souris and Le Hanneton, another 'female' bar. There he started working on the portrait of his friend Paul Leclercq and completed his plans for the well-known album of twelve lithographs called *Elles* – six of which were adapted from earlier oil paintings. Its enlarged frontispiece was to be used as a poster for the exhibition of the album on the premises of *La Plume*. With the exception of Cha-U-Kao, *'elles'* were the prostitutes whom Lautrec captured in the simplicity of their 'private' lives. Only one 'client' was represented in a picture which was renamed *The Woman in a Corset* instead of the original *A Passing Conquest*, in order to make the scene more anodyne. Casting a completely impas-

sive gaze, all the images represented the usually unknown intimacy of everyday life in the brothels (page 126). The naturalism of gestures and postures did not induce voyeurism, but rather invited the viewer's complicity in calmly sharing the moments portrayed. These were presented for themselves rather than as propaganda pieces serving to buttress a moral interpretation. Once again, Lautrec refused to pass judgement and the title of *Elles* referred to women in general as much as to the 'professionals' – whom he decidedly refused to represent as curious beasts on the margins of society.

The album was commissioned by the publisher Pellet and in the five colour plates – the others were printed on white or tinted backgrounds – Lautrec displayed a taste for shades and half-tones which contrasted with the violent flat colours for which he had shown a preference in most of his earlier graphic works. The drawing became lighter: what was lost of its nervousness was compensated by its evocative power. In spite of all these qualities, the album was a commercial failure and Pellet had to decide in the end to break it up and sell the plates individually. The series had obviously disappointed lovers of erotic scenes and smutty pictures, which was their loss.

During the autumn of 1898 Lautrec started showing signs of instability which increasingly worried his relations. Completely intoxicated, worn out by the nights of drinking at the end of which he often had to be brought home, he became very irritable and prone to outbursts of unjustified anger. In spite of all this, he illustrated the *Histoires naturelles* by the novelist Jules Renard and spent long days at the Zoological Gardens engaged in research. The book appeared the following year – it was another failure.

In January 1899 his mother, who had to leave Paris unexpectedly, asked her trusted old housekeeper Berthe Sarrazin to keep an eye on Henri and the apartment in the rue de Douai. He took this sudden departure very badly and considered it a grave betrayal. The daily reports which Berthe included in her letters to the countess document the painter's activities and the progressive decline of his mental health. He spent his money on useless purchases, accumulating knick-knacks, cake moulds, dolls, 'all kinds of old junk' – until he decided to give everything away to his friends. In his studio, where he had more and more trouble sleeping, he complained about being attacked by different animals and a huge number of microbes. He spent a lot of his time rubbing his paintings with glycerine, causing Berthe and Lautrec's friends to express fears that the artist might ruin his work. With Calmèse, a neighbour who owned a stable and rented out horses, he regularly got extremely drunk. He suffered from memory loss, his moods alternated between aggression and kindness, he had fears of persecution, 'changed his opinions twenty times in two minutes' and 'did not work at all'.

Along with his thirst, his appetite for women did not diminish. On one occasion, after receiving a loan of 1,000 francs from his cousin Gabriel, Lautrec spent a night in a hotel with 'another gentleman and two women of ill repute'. The following morning, having squandered all of the money, he had nothing left with which to pay the hotel bill. He could only shout 'I am the count of Toulouse', and barely avoided being taken away to the police station. The unfortunate Berthe Sarrazin was at her wits' end. She had no way to plan his meals: sometimes he brought guests for dinner without advance warning, on other occasions he forgot to come to eat. He claimed he was being robbed, suspected everyone of engaging in intrigues behind his back, rejected any advice, decided never to come back to the rue de Douai as long as his mother was absent, then returned in order to take away some of her knick-knacks and silverware. At the beginning of February his mother hired a male nurse, but he proved to be incapable of looking after him properly and, above all, of making him stop drinking. In March, upon his mother's instructions and against the artist's own will, Lautrec had to be interned in the hospital in Neuilly after having a fit in one of the

Coqs, *1899.*
Lithograph illustration for
Histoires Naturelles *by Jules Renard.*
Josefowitz Collection

brothels in the rue des Moulins. Lautrec found himself 'surrounded by mad people'. As soon as he recovered, he started thinking about leaving and proving to his mother that his internment had not been justified. He asked Joyant to get hold of his drawing materials, hoping to show that he was normal and that his creative abilities were intact – especially to mediocre journalists who had informed Parisians that this adventure was a just and predictable conclusion to a disorderly body of work largely concentrated on the degrading aspects of human existence. The thirty-nine drawings devoted to the circus, entirely based on memories, showed an obsessive desire to discover the secret of movement, of life-force. When they were exhibited at the Toulouse-Lautrec retrospective in 1931, the artist André Lhote, who until then had had only 'a moderate esteem' for

At the circus – performing horse and monkey, 1899.
Black chalk, coloured crayons and graphite, 44 × 26.7 cm
Private Collection

Lautrec's work, revised his judgement. He expressed his unreserved admiration for the mastery with which the painter 'tried hard to restore to these shapes, once emptied of their content, the major elements of which he had deprived them. The bodies swelled and became round, the light became brighter, the outlines sharper. The emptiness exists only in between the figures.' Furthermore, Lhote did not hesitate to compare the series with Dürer, Daumier or Goya.[29]

Lautrec left the clinic at the end of May 1899. He managed to draw and paint there, in particular the portraits of other internees, his nurse, dogs and horses. His work from this period combines something of his sinister present condition with adolescent themes: as the seats in the circus were almost empty in all of the drawings, so the trained dogs, Footit on his knees in front of the ringmaster, the tamer or the tightrope walker all perform only for themselves, without expecting any applause, and Cha-U-Kao, with her permanently impassive features, performs somersaults on the ground with a donkey, concentrating only on her self-centred enjoyment.

Once he had been released, Lautrec was given a 'keeper': Paul Viaud, an impoverished distant relative without an occupation, was given the responsibility of following him everywhere. At first it seemed as if the painter had changed; he did not drink any more, or hardly at all. He left for the Bassin d'Arcachon in July and, while in Le Havre, discovered the Star, a sailors' bar where the waitress fascinated him so much that he had to ask Joyant to send his painting kit to him urgently (page 131). That autumn, after his return to Paris, Lautrec resumed his work and once again took up his well-rehearsed themes. The lithographs proliferated: race-course scenes, *The Jockey* (page 133), horses which he observed in Calmèse's stables, dogs, and yet more clowns. Nevertheless, his health was not good and he was again tempted by alcohol. Soon he took up the habit again, concealing the drink in a hollowed walking stick which could contain up to half a litre of liquid.

It was 1900, all Paris was rushing to the Universal Exhibition. Lautrec, who refused a place on the hanging committee, replied to a request from Frantz Toussaint to exhibit his graphics: 'I refuse categorically if there is to be a jury.' He visited the exhibition in a bath-chair and returned exhausted, but full of enthusiasm for the Japanese section. In May Joyant took him to the Somme estuary (page 135). He then spent some time with his mother at the château de Malromé and afterwards rented a studio in Bordeaux, where he was entranced by the performances he saw there of *Messaline*, 'a lyrical tragedy in 4 acts and 5 scenes'. He devoted six canvases to the spectacle, rendering the luxurious ambience of decadence which enchanted him so much with a soft drawing style and unusual use of impasto. These new stylistic traits contribute to strangely static works, almost emphatic in their attempt at solemnity. Not even the colours are persuasive, in spite of the daring combinations of red and green. The paintings are dominated by an atmosphere redolent of the end of a reign, but, in spite of what Lautrec believed,[30] they symbolized more the end of his art than that of the Roman Empress, even though *Messaline* (E. Bührle Collection, Zurich) has been perceived as a precursor of Expressionism.

Lautrec spent that winter in Bordeaux, and a part of it in Taussat, but his mother brought him back to Malromé, because he had fallen ill. He lost weight, had to spend time in bed, and found it hard to move around. Only in May 1901 did he manage to get back to Paris with Viaud. He saw his friends once more, rearranged his studio and put his initials on his canvases and drawings. He was prone to depression but rejoiced to learn that the price of his works was going up. But why stay in Paris? The motive which had stimulated his painting was gone. In July in Arcachon he did not manage to finish *An Examination at the Medical Faculty in Paris* (page 139) nor, a month later, was he able to complete the great parodic portrait of his 'guardian' Viaud dressed as an admiral, in a powdered wig and the uniform of an eighteenth-century British naval officer.

Invitation to an exhibition, *1898.*
Lithograph
Musée Toulouse-Lautrec, Albi

Henri de Toulouse-Lautrec died on 9 September 1901 in his mother's castle at Malromé. His death had been brought about by his congenital malady, aggravated by the effects of syphilis, years of excessive drinking and relentless dedication to his work. After a working life of less than twenty years, Lautrec had left a substantial artistic legacy, consisting of no less than 737 oil paintings, well over 5,000 drawings, more than 300 prints and some 275 watercolours. The artist's words to his friend Arthur Huc several years before his death, at the age of only thirty-six, have a tragically ironic ring: 'I can paint until I am forty. From then on, I intend to be completely drained.' Despite the brevity of his life, Lautrec's impact not only on the art world of *fin-de-siècle* Paris, but also on the counter-culture of Montmartre, of which he was the most celebrated chronicler, had been considerable. Such was the presence of Lautrec and his work that we might justifiably ask whether the popular art forms which flourished in the cabarets of the period would have enjoyed such lasting fame had it not been for the distinctive body of imagery he created.

In the year that saw Lautrec's death, Picasso painted *The Blue Room*, in which a naked woman performs her toilette in a tub. On the wall in the background hangs Lautrec's poster of May Milton, with which the young Spanish artist had decorated his studio upon his arrival in Paris.

At Lautrec's funeral, Count Alphonse took the driver's seat on the hearse, 'to see that his Henri was driven to his last resting place like a gentleman'. He whipped the horses and made everyone in the procession run after them – anticipating a famous sequence from René Clair's film *Entr'acte*.

In October 1901 Lautrec's father wrote to Joyant conferring on him the role of executor of his son's artistic legacy and explaining his own attitude towards the body of work he had left: 'I do not intend to be converted now that he is dead, and to sing the praises of what I could only understand, while he was alive, as brave and daring sketches.' He concluded by saying: 'You have greater faith in this work than I do,

and you are right.' Having thus been entrusted with the responsibility for Lautrec's posthumous fame, Maurice Joyant worked hard to make the painter better known. He organized a retrospective exhibition in 1914, for which he managed to gather together as many as 202 works from many private collections. In the preface to the catalogue for this exhibition, Arsène Alexandre, the art critic and one of the painter's most devoted advocates, expressed his hope that one day he 'would be able to explore in depth the philosophical and artistic goldmine which is his work, so closely linked to his thought. But on the occasion of today's definitive exhibition of his œuvre, which already gives us an overview of that thinking, I am determined to claim, both for the man and for the painter, their proper place and worth.'

However, Joyant's main contribution to the artist's enduring fame and presence in the public's eye was the foundation of the Lautrec Museum in Albi. He persuaded the Countess Adèle to donate her collection of her son's works to his birthplace so that it could be displayed in the old bishop's palace, the Palais de la Berbie, which stands in the shadow of the town's celebrated cathedral. Setting up the Lautrec collection in the museum at Albi was a long and arduous job, however, only brought to a successful conclusion thanks to the energy and devotion of the artist's friends, Maurice Joyant, Arsène Alexandre and Gabriel Tapié de Céleyran, the last of whom was responsible for originally devising the idea in 1907. Upon its completion in 1922, writing in a letter to Joyant, Countess Adèle de Toulouse-Lautrec expressed her 'complete satisfaction' at this enterprise 'to the glory of Henri'.

1864 ❧ 1901

THE PLATES

Lautrec painted this oil on cardboard when he was
only sixteen. It is his only 'classical' self-portrait
and was to be followed by a series of caricatures,
silhouettes of the artist's back (page 65) or the almost
anonymous inclusion of himself as an extra at the
edges of some of the bigger compositions (page 95).
Here he has represented his head and shoulders,
reflected in a mirror above a fireplace. He appears,
not as an adolescent, but rather as a young adult,
severe and almost disturbed by the image he has
discovered of himself. In order to get to this image, it
is necessary to go beyond the obstacles placed in the
foreground: boxes and pots, which occupy as much of
the canvas as its principal subject and thus isolate and
symbolically protect the sitter. This self-portrait
allows only an exterior – that is, a superficial – grasp
of the subject, who keeps tight hold of the secrets of
his inner self.

The broad brushstroke and the unusual layout is
already remarkable: we can anticipate what kind of
portrait painter the artist was to become. We are
tempted to discover prematurely in this early work
the mastery which Lautrec was to acquire progressively in the following years.

There is evidence to suggest that this painting was
never exhibited publicly during the artist's lifetime.
His mother discovered it somewhere at the back of his
studio and gave it to the Musée d'Albi in 1922.

Self-Portrait

Painted 1880
40.5 × 32.5 cm
Musée Toulouse-Lautrec, Albi

Among numerous equestrian scenes painted by Lautrec in the early years of his career, this dog-cart is particularly successful: the young painter proved himself attentive to Princeteau's instructions (the older painter commented that his young student was able to 'imitate like a little ape') and the example of Lewis-Brown.

While the composition is extremely simple, with the subject carefully centred, the treatment of leaves by a series of broad brushstrokes this time resolved Lautrec's usual difficulties with the details of the landscape. We can also distinguish the subtle play of colour: the blue seen through a gap in the greenery, and, on the left, delicately recalling the tone of the driver's trousers, the horizontal surface of the pond and the luminous area on the right. The artist has used an interesting range of techniques here: the wheels and the harnessing testify to quick brushstrokes, the vehicle itself is made out of just a few lines of pigment, while the horse and the human figures are painted in a more subtle fashion. Since the vehicle is not in motion, Lautrec gives a feel of energy to the composition through the postures of the two men and the horse's right hind leg. The shade carefully placed in the foreground stops the scene from appearing too posed and artificial.

A Dog-Cart

Painted 1880
27 × 35 cm
Musée Toulouse-Lautrec, Albi

Soon after entering Bonnat's studio, Lautrec had to prove his ability by producing a painting which would appeal to the dominant taste of the day. Indeed, this nude could not shock anyone because neither its posture – chaste and almost meditative – nor its pictorial technique suggests the revelation of a hidden truth. The delicate tones, the contrast between the pale flesh, the black hair and stockings (which do not, in any way, appear provocative), and well-outlined profile indicate that, from an academic point of view, the nude had to correspond to a preconceived aesthetic idea (this was a classical 'theme' which should have been treated just like a history scene, an interior genre subject or a still-life composition), rather than affirm a specific physical existence. In this case, however, the originality of the artist's conception once more lends a new lease of life to a traditional theme.

The couch is rendered more freely through the way the painter conveys its decorative motifs, and the cushions, on the left, are painted with quicker brushstrokes. As this was a 'study', the model was given pride of place and the artist was quite correct in rather neglecting the background. The rug which covers the couch also appears in Rachou's portrait of Lautrec, painted a year later.

Study of a Nude

Painted 1882
55 × 46 cm
Musée Toulouse-Lautrec, Albi

enri Rachou (1855–1944) was the son of a banker from Lautrec's home town, Albi. He was instrumental in helping the artist to gain admission as a student with Bonnat. This portrait, painted around the same time as the preceding nude, provides a contrast to the texture of that work, because here the artist uses a more 'Impressionist' brushstroke which does not blend in an over-polished image, but rather takes over as the basic element. Lautrec also favoured a more luminous atmosphere in which the canvas being painted by Rachou attracts the viewer's attention in a two-fold way, both through its near-monopoly of the colour blue and by the manner in which it is detached from the dark areas of the background. In this way the painter Rachou becomes paradoxically less important than his painting: the centre of the painting is taken up by his hand rather than his face. To paint another painter is to produce a form of displaced self-portrait by evoking the occupation shared with the sitter. If, however, we follow the way in which the easel crosses the edges of the canvas while the human figure is inscribed in it without any difficulty, we can conclude that the work still proved to be a problem to Lautrec.

The Painter, Rachou

Painted 1882
50 × 61 cm
Private collection

With Carmen Gaudin, Lautrec's attraction to red-haired women becomes obvious. In a letter to his mother he mentioned painting the portrait of a woman 'whose hair is all gold'. She was not a professional model, but a worker. It appears that Lautrec accosted her in the street one day in the presence of Rachou and invited her to pose for him in his studio. She was the subject of four of the portraits he painted in 1885, a series of works which marked an important turning-point in the evolution of his style and technique. Later on, Carmen modelled for a number of other Montmartre artists, but Lautrec lost interest in her when her hair turned a darker shade of brown. On the back of this painting she is represented with her head lowered, so that her bright red hair becomes the central motif on which the play of light is concentrated. The frill of her blouse was not reproduced in the other versions, but its allusive treatment here balances the care brought to the details of her face – and the memory of Bonnat's and Cormon's teaching surfaces again.

Carmen Gaudin was later to pose for other paintings in which her whole silhouette acquired growing importance: for example, the portrait 'in the white working jacket' (1888), in which Lautrec, unusually for him, elaborated the details of the room furnishings. *Montrouge. Rosa la Rouge* (based on a Bruant song about the prostitute Rosa the Redhead, who lured men into dark doorways where her accomplice would rob and kill them) again features Carmen, this time transformed, by the evocative title, into a 'realist' figure. She was also the model for *The Laundress*, where the painter brought together the many lessons he had learnt (on light, silhouette and contrasts) at the precise moment when he formed his own, personal mode of expression. By 1885, the basis of Lautrec's art was established.

Carmen, The Red-Head

Painted 1885
23.9 × 15 cm
Musée Toulouse-Lautrec, Albi

Contrary to the usual practice at the time, Lautrec did not copy works by the great masters. Nevertheless, he occasionally appropriated his well-known contemporaries, either in an open parody (as in *The Sacred Grove* by 'Pubis de Cheval') or in a simplifying gesture, as was the case with this painting, inspired by a work painted in 1869 by Alfred Stevens (1823–1906), an academic painter who enjoyed a great reputation. These two borrowings gave him an opportunity to produce large-scale paintings, something which was still unusual for him at that time.

Lautrec concentrated his attention on the two protagonists, neglecting the furniture and the subsidiary characters. This conferred a central visual impact on his study of the drapery, and his chromatic harmonies could well rival bourgeois Salon paintings. At the same time, the canvas becomes strangely disoriented, because of the absence of a title which could define the roles played by the characters. At the same time, the woman's legs might be thought to appear too long. This interpretation of Stevens's painting functions at one and the same time as a homage and as a gesture of Lautrec distancing himself from a particular pictorial tradition. This departure from the *bon ton* is noticeable in the cramped fingers (a negative prefiguring of Yvette Guilbert's gloves) and in the framing of the face with red hair: the portrait, Lautrec seems to be suggesting here, is something other after all than merely a fashionable drawing.

In the Studio. The Model's Pose

Painted c.1885
140 × 55 cm
Musée des Beaux-Arts, Lille

If we compare this portrait of a fellow student from the studio of Cormon (to whom Lautrec was never very close, maybe because he found him too theoretical in his interests) with that of Carmen Gaudin (page 53), we can easily perceive the evolution in his style. The use of a light background gives the figure a new presence, and Lautrec shows himself capable of using the skill he has acquired (which is very visible in the way the hair is painted) to define himself as a 'modern' painter. In his memoirs, Bernard revealed that Lautrec 'spent twenty sittings on it and could not make the background fit the face'. The brushstrokes show great sensibility, the modelling of the face is effective (even though the light appears too even) and the pose looks natural. This canvas is no doubt indebted to Renoir, whose manner of painting the lips of his models Lautrec greatly admired. Bernard's mouth is particularly well painted; it relies simultaneously on the shades of the background and the reflection which, coming from a button, confirms the vertical organization of the painting.

Portrait of Emile Bernard

Painted 1885
54.5 × 43.5 cm
Tate Gallery, London

Lautrec did not get involved in the theoretical debates about painting so common in the artistic milieu in which he was trained; he preferred to judge these theories by their results and kept only the parts which interested him. This also describes his attitude towards Impressionism, which is apparent in this third portrait he painted of his mother, and which he prepared by a rather academic charcoal sketch made in 1885. He partially relied on the Impressionists' techniques while at the same time criticizing them in an indirect way. Thus the care he devotes to the décor (the furniture, tapestries, fireplace in the background) keeps the stress on those elements of drawing which the Impressionists tend to neglect, while the paint is only used in fine layers through which the texture of the base appears. The same is true for the illusion of depth which Lautrec reintroduced in this painting, defining it through an almost classical system of perspective. The room is seen from an angled viewpoint directed into the corner, with the light coming from two separate sources: the window and its reflection in a mirror. As for the maternal figure, tender and affectionate, she is nevertheless detached from her surroundings, firmly established in the foreground, elaborated with an autonomous, albeit softened chromaticity, and her outline does not dissolve at all in the light effects.

Between 1879 and 1886 Lautrec, who had a very close and affectionate relationship with his mother, painted numerous portraits of the countess, in different techniques and formats. In this one (which used to hang in the drawing-room at Malromé, the house she loved best, having chosen and decorated it herself), absorbed in her reading, she does not reveal any part of her soul: probably this lack of psychological ambition allowed Lautrec to attempt a new and previously unseen pictorial synthesis.

The Countess Adèle de Toulouse-Lautrec in the Drawing-Room at Malromé

Painted 1887
59 × 54 cm
Musée Toulouse-Lautrec, Albi

*T*he Quadrille of the Louis-Treize Chair at the *Elysée Montmartre*, from 1886, marked the first appearance of non-classical ballet dancers in Lautrec's oil paintings. In his second painting of cabaret life, La Goulue became the archetype of the new dancer. Lautrec tried to seize both the significant attitudes and characteristic physiognomies – hence the importance of his use of monochromatic paint on partially uncovered cardboard. Diluted oil paint gave the energy of a quick sketch to the painting, but this did not stop the work from underlining the interesting contrast of the silhouettes and giving added importance to La Goulue's skirts, balanced by the white surface on which the two heads were outlined. The few lines indicating the floor-boards are enough to establish a sense of perspective while the spectators who witness the scene remain undifferentiated.

The same year Lautrec completed another painting on cardboard devoted to a very similar theme (*At the Moulin de la Galette*, Hahnloser Collection, Winthertur) in which the chromaticity of the décor is more detailed, an effect achieved at the expense of some of the impact in the artist's rendition of the couple dancing.

At the Moulin de la Galette.
La Goulue and Valentin le Désossé

Painted 1887
52 × 39.2 cm
Musée Toulouse-Lautrec, Albi

In 1887 Lautrec completed a portrait of van Gogh in which he displayed the ability to adopt the style of his fellow student in Cormon's studio. The same year – when he also painted the portrait of his mother (page 59) in which we noticed the partial influence of Impressionism – saw the realization of another portrait indicating that his active stylistic research was not finished: this oil painting of Madame Alice Gibert. This search for an original style was only to be completed once Lautrec took up the range of specific themes which today have come to be so widely associated with his way of painting. The originality of style had to go together with an originality of motif.

This is obviously a portrait of a very honourable lady with impeccable manners: the design of the table and the care taken in painting the details both of the décor and of the other objects are signs of Lautrec's readiness to produce a portrait that would not shock the sitter herself, who is treated with sympathy. The light is not so sharp as to lead to any distortion of the features, and the facial expression of the woman, absorbed by her reading, is gentle. The brushstrokes, which lead in all directions across the rear wall, take on a more disciplined feel in the treatment of the chair, particularly where they follow the cut of the dress – which is highlighted by touches of the same intense shade of red found on the carpet.

If he had followed in the direction indicated by this portrait, Lautrec could have become a 'conventional' artist, possibly somewhat lacking in personality, but able to find a clientele of art lovers ready to accept a limited amount of discreet daring and a reassuring command of pictorial technique.

Madame Alice Gibert

Painted 1887
61 × 50 cm
Private collection

In September 1886 Lautrec published in *Le Courrier Français* (a weekly founded two years previously and aimed predominantly at the middle-class public) a drawing which is quite similar to this painting, with the exception of the two normal-sized characters who are shown sitting on the bar stools in the left-hand side of the drawing. Here he represented himself standing, barely reaching to the level of the bar: it is quite likely that the other client is Valentin le Désossé, who featured in so many of Lautrec's paintings of cabaret scenes. This self-portrait symbolically completes an oil painting of the same size dating from 1884, *Self-Portrait from the Back* (M. Klingman Collection), in which the painter is shown standing in front of his easel: his existence is thus represented as being divided between the activities of painting and drinking. In spite of its apparent theme, *At the Bar* tilts the scale in favour of the former occupation, since, in pictorial terms, the mere presence of the little silhouette of the artist is enough to even out the group of three characters on the right of the canvas.

At the Bar

Painted 1887
55 × 42 cm
Mellon Collection, Upperville, Virginia

The model, a seventeen-year-old neighbour of the artist, inspired Lautrec to paint several portraits in 1888 (others can be seen in the Kunsthalle, Bremen and the Musée du Louvre). This version is the closest in appearance to a photograph of Hélène Vary that was taken during the same year by the artist's friend François Gauzi. (It was not uncommon for Lautrec to use a photograph as a basis for his portraits.) The back of the armchair, together with the pile of stretchers and canvases which fills the background, obviously indicates that the sittings took place in the studio, but its primary purpose is to even out the composition and underline the model's bust; without it, the face alone would attract the viewer's gaze. If we could compare the face on the painting with the one shown on the photograph, we would see that it is not a caricature – though this has been claimed all too often – but a characterization stressing the modesty and distinction of the model. The profile attracts all the light and Lautrec applies to it an extremely refined chromatic treatment, different from the quick and streaky brushstrokes which make up the dress and the background.

This painting was first exhibited at the prestigious Cercle Volney, either in 1890 or a year later, alongside portraits by the most fashionable painters of the day, such as Lautrec's old teacher Léon Bonnat and Jean-Jacques Henner. After the exhibition, as he informed his mother in a letter, he sold the picture and received 200 francs for it, once the dealer had deducted his commission.

Hélène Vary

Painted 1888
54.8 × 29.5 cm
Musée Toulouse-Lautrec, Albi

This *grisaille* on cardboard is one of the three made to illustrate an article by Emile Michelet on life in Paris during the summer (when everyone who could had left town) which appeared in *Le Paris illustré* on 7 July 1888. This was a rather lavishly produced magazine with a chic bourgeois circulation. The two remaining *grisailles* (a technique Lautrec favoured for his illustrations, most likely because of the speed with which they could be reproduced) represented *The Driver of the Omnibus Company* (in which there is a self-portrait from the back) and the *Riders going to the Bois de Boulogne*. Although this was merely a project for an illustration, Lautrec worked with as much care as if it were for a painting, possibly because this was going to be his first publication in a journal other than Bruant's *Le Mirliton*.

Here his friend Gauzi plays the father of the family in a scene of subtle, but real irony on the petit-bourgeois way of life and its social pretentions. The sitter's recollections give us an insight into Lautrec's attitudes: 'Posing for Lautrec is almost a pleasure. He was not exacting and did not insist on absolute immobility. We chatted away as time flew, and were enlivened by his off-the-cuff wit, his funny jokes and his good humour.' The painting was finished in a day, the other figures having been invented to fit the social stereotypes: the plump mother, the self-satisfied adolescent, and so on.

The walk appears a joyless affair, a ritual by now lacking any meaning (one just needs to think of contemporary celebrations of religious life – the First Communion was a regular subject in academic painting). The choice of the shop window represented in the work was partly determined by the need to have more white for reproduction purposes, but the presence of the row of white shirts adds to the rigidity of the father and thus, as if through some visual contagion, the whole family appears stiff.

First Communion Day

Painted 1888
61 × 36 cm
Musée des Augustins, Toulouse

This is a crucial work in Lautrec's evolution as a painter, not only because it is the first large composition devoted to a subject from circus life, but because it attempts to represent characters involved in divergent activities in the very space which the artist needed to elaborate as a gathering-point for these figures. The red of the curving ringside neatly separates the riding arena from the audience and serves to structure the composition. It also confers on the bareback rider and her grey-violet horse the power to attract the viewer's gaze, while the gesture of the ringmaster Mr Loyal – and his cropped figure – provide a counterpoint.

As a result of the elevated point of view, a large part of the circus and many of its audience fall outside the ambit of our gaze and all of the figures (the clowns and the audience) have been cropped by the frame, a feature which only adds to the impression of generalized movement. The rider, whose face and red hair are outlined against the green surface of the partition, is depicted in the moment just before another acrobatic leap, a jump through the paper ring held out by one of the clowns. The horse itself, in a foreshortened perspective, suggests the possibility rather than the actual use of energy.

The colour in this painting tends – at least partially – towards flat tint, anticipating the artist's use of it in the posters. We should therefore not be surprised to learn that this canvas was bought by Charles Zidler and was hung, in 1889, on the right-hand side of the entrance hall of the Moulin Rouge. The painting had already been favourably received by Theo van Rysselberghe, who had begun to scout in Paris in late 1887 for the Brussels exhibition society, Les XX. Lautrec showed it at their fifth exhibition, together with some portraits.

At the Cirque Fernando: The Ringmaster

Painted 1888
98 × 61 cm
The Art Institute of Chicago

This oil painting on cardboard has conventionally been said to date from a later period (based on Joyant, who allocated it to 1896), but recent research has placed its composition seven years earlier. This new dating is based on the evidence of Lautrec's letter to an art dealer in 1890, in which he unambiguously describes this painting and another – of similar size, handling and colour – which features the same model: *The Toilette: The Model's Rest*. Since the style of both paintings evokes that of Degas's pastels, we can safely assume that they were painted in response to the pastels of female models which were exhibited by Degas in 1886 and 1888.

Differing from Lautrec's usual treatment, the cardboard is completely covered in paint: the placing of the semi-nude body within its surroundings seems to have challenged Lautrec, providing the artist as it does with an opportunity to display considerable tonal subtlety. Otherwise, Lautrec maintains his habitually neutral gaze: as the model is seen from the back and treated with the utmost respect and modesty, the viewer cannot be reproached with indiscretion. As no preliminary studies for this work survive, we can assume that it was painted directly from life. The high viewpoint allows the spectator implicitly to dominate the model, who is sitting on the floor. It all seems as if the vision offered to the viewer was the result of an unexpected chance, which the painter has attempted to reconstruct in all its freshness. This is one of the basic ingredients of Lautrec's art: a pursuit of the most fleeting forms of beauty – part of the artist's quest for the 'natural' source of life itself making the viewer forget that a model has posed before him.

The Toilette (Red-Head)

Painted 1889
67 × 54 cm
Musée d'Orsay, Paris

Between 1890 and 1896 the Moulin Rouge was the inspiration for about thirty of Lautrec's oil paintings, all of which centred more on the public and the stars than on the architecture of the dance hall; the painter was much more interested in people.

In this painting – the third most important after *At the Cirque Fernando* and *At the Moulin de la Galette* of 1889 – the characters are neatly grouped in three categories which organize the space. The public at the back, whose hats outline a frieze on the wall – which would later be portrayed more schematically in the poster of 1891 (page 79) – define the background. At the centre of the space the impassive figure of Valentin and his dancing partner are multiplied by the strange shadows spreading on the ground. In the foreground, two women and a masculine silhouette are cut by the border of the canvas. This division is twice negated, by the diagonal line which connects the woman in pink with the dancer's stockings and the red waistcoat of the groom on the left, and also by the visual contiguity of the planes, in which the dancers appear to be surrounded by the audience – despite the fact that very few looks are really turned towards their movements. The complexity of the composition and the exploration in colour confirm the maturity of the painter, but they substitute the pleasure of painting for the pleasures of celebrating. This form of art bases its pleasure principle upon a spectacle in which none of its participants feels any joy.

Dance at the Moulin Rouge

Painted 1890
115 × 150 cm
Philadelphia Museum of Art

In most of his portraits, Lautrec did not search for an original pose; the model, most often not a professional one, is represented in profile, semi-profile or full face against a neutral background such as the corner of the artist's studio, inside a room, or sometimes in front of distant foliage. His standing portraits of revellers (page 113) are an exception to this rule.

Casque d'Or represents a typical character from the dregs of society; a prostitute, she was the mistress of an anarchist who was executed by the guillotine. She embodies all that 'respectable society' rejects. For Lautrec, however, she is first and foremost a female figure, a fact which guarantees her as much of the painter's attention as would be devoted by him to a portrait of any other woman. This is especially the case in relation to her hairdo (which was the inspiration for her nickname, 'Golden Helmet', and was so popular that many dancers wore wigs imitating her hair style) and her impenetrable face, which does not give away any of her secrets.

This portrait expresses neither condescension nor admiration; it concentrates on fixing the exact image which the prostitute is ready to give of herself: a little mouth, a direct gaze and pale make-up, all of which are at one and the same time imitated and undermined by Lautrec's hatchings. Outlined with a vigorous line, the half-figure is placed in the foreground as if the garden were merely one of those illusionist canvases used by photographers; different from the more conventional artists who paid attention to nature, Lautrec turned it into a set design.

The Streetwalker (or Casque d'Or)

Painted 1891
64.7 × 53 cm
Philadelphia Museum of Art

'The paradigm of the modern poster', according to Félix Fénéon, this poster was conceived for the Moulin Rouge at the request of its owner. It was meant to replace an earlier one by Chéret on which pleasant-looking young women enjoyed a donkey ride in front of the Moulin's wings. Lautrec sought his inspiration in a different direction, in the work of Bonnard (his *France-Champage* was completed the same year), and in the Japanese prints which circulated in the artistic milieu. He retained from the latter the importance of black silhouettes – which were also influenced by the projections of 'Chinese shades' at Le Chat Noir, with which he was familiar – as well as the arrangement of postures and the role of simplified decorative elements.

La Goulue here acts out her double role, just as in the Moulin Rouge itself: she is at the head of the poster, both through her name and by her movement, which places the whiteness of her undergarments in the centre of the image. Valentin, who is treated in the foreground like a shadow and defined with a few decisive lines, establishes a contrast to La Goulue and at the same time creates a false symmetry in relation to the row of silhouettes in top hats. If we compare the final sketch (see page 23) which was preceded by numerous studies, in particular of La Goulue's head) with the definitive poster, we can observe the importance of the artist's final corrections: the re-orientation of the lines of perspective, the reduction of the yellow shapes (the Chinese lanterns) on the left to pure surface, and the continuity of the public in the background.

While this poster guaranteed its author almost instantaneous fame, and gave him the opportunity to reach a public which had not known him beforehand, it also gave rise to the over-determining myth of Lautrec 'the painter of Montmartre'.

The Moulin Rouge — La Goulue

Printed 1891
170 × 130 cm
Musée Toulouse-Lautrec, Albi

The Dihau family, originally from Lille, was distantly related to the Toulouse-Lautrecs. In the years 1890–1 Lautrec completed several portraits of the two brothers Henri and Désiré (who was the bassoonist in the orchestra at the Paris opera house) and of their sister Marie, who taught music and gave singing lessons. The family were friends of Degas, who had painted Marie's portrait and whose painting *The Musicians in the Orchestra* (1868), featuring Désiré playing a bassoon, decorated the family apartment. Lautrec greatly admired the work and it seems that it was Marie who first introduced him to Degas.

Few of Lautrec's friends were depicted more frequently than Désiré Dihau. Whereas his brother Henri was represented standing, like a respectable petit-bourgeois happy to be alive, and in Lautrec's other portrait, which is three times larger, Désiré Dihau is shown reading newspapers in his garden, this portrait is the most modest one of the series. This small oil painting has no other pretentions than to express the affection the painter felt towards his model and friend. Désiré Dihau had a double career as an official musician at the Opéra and as a writer of light songs. Lautrec also illustrated some of these songs and made a lithograph portrait of Désiré. During the same year he made his first portrait of their sister Marie at the piano, which was shown at the sixth Salon des Indépendants, where it was admired by van Gogh.

Désiré Dihau, Bassoonist at the Opéra

Painted 1891
35 × 27 cm
Musée Toulouse-Lautrec, Albi

Lautrec felt a genuine fascination for women's hair: we have already observed this in his treatment of Carmen Gaudin's red hair, the knot on top of La Goulue's head, and, as we shall see again later, Jane Avril's hair. He also elaborated scenes of combing and curling hair as rare gestures which represent particular moments in the transition between the privacy of the toilette and the public space for which the hairdo is being made. In 1891 he devoted at least five paintings to this theme. In one of them, *Two Women in Shirts curling their Hair* (Saõ Paulo Museum), dedicated to the sculptor Carabin, a homosexual relationship is also being suggested.

The face of this *Woman Combing Her Hair* caught as it is in a half-bent position, is not visible to the spectator: the only important thing to see is the flowing hair itself. This anonymous approach was to be repeated in three other paintings on the same theme (*Women Combing Their Hair, The One who is Combing* and *Woman Curling Her Hair*). Another important element in this painting is the grace of the woman's unselfconscious gesture and above all the act of capturing an intimate moment, which is also suggested by the complementary décor.

Woman Combing Her Hair

Painted 1891
43 × 30 cm
Musée d'Orsay, Paris

The collaboration with Bruant reached its peak with this poster, which is even more explosive than the one for the Moulin Rouge (page 78). Relying solely on large surfaces of violently contrasting colours, Lautrec stressed the energetic stature of the singer, underlined – apart from the entertainer's customary attributes such as the red scarf, the dark cape, the wide-brimmed hat and the knobbly walking-stick – by the central figure's effective backwards-leaning posture. The massive body, represented without any graphic details, offers a contrast to the firmly drawn face, itself a real portrait. In the background, the shadow of the engine operator (yet another borrowing from Japanese prints) is enough to suggest the perspective. The lettering itself is more effective than for the Moulin Rouge poster.

In spite of its obvious impact, Ducarre, the owner of Les Ambassadeurs, one of the most elegant *cafés-concerts* on the Champs-Elysées, wanted to reject the poster. Bruant, on the other hand, was enthusiastic and had to threaten to cancel his singing tour in order to have the poster displayed on both sides of the stage as well as all over the walls of Paris.

By means of a simple inversion, the same design was later used with some variations as a layout for Bruant's performances in another cabaret, the Eldorado. The following year, Lautrec produced two other equally remarkable posters. The first one (*Aristide Bruant in his Cabaret*, in which the singer is represented in profile) was to figure in the 1896 exhibition of artistic posters at the Cirque de Reims. It was also reproduced in *La Plume*, in 1896 and again three years later, in 1899. The second one (*Aristide Bruant at Le Mirliton*) shows the singer from the back, dressed in black velvet and black boots: the silhouette was so famous that the face no longer had to be shown.

Aristide Bruant at Les Ambassadeurs

Printed 1892
150 × 100 cm
Bibliothèque nationale, Paris

AMBASSADEURS
aristide
BRUANT
dans
son cabaret
HLautrec
IMP EDW ANCOURT & Cie 83 Fg St DENIS

This poster was designed to announce the publication of a serial called *Les Drames de Toulouse* by A. Siegel, in the journal *La Dépêche* and thus there was no need for an accompanying text. The necessary information was printed on separate strips of paper and fixed independently, either above or below the image.

Here, Lautrec turned to his advantage a technical limitation: he was allowed to use only one colour for the printing, and he could exploit the possibilities of the background white to underline the dramatic effects of his composition. The candlelight deforms the hanged man's features and turns him into a phantom-like presence, stressing his shirt in particular. The format of the image, which suggested the use of vertical lines, led Lautrec to turn them in an oblique angle: the space which he represents thus conjures up a nightmare and the hanged man appears to be swinging. Such an arrangement prefigures, at least in part, the expressionist treatment of similar themes, especially the kind of Expressionism which appeared in the German cinema some thirty years later.

The Hanged Man

Printed 1892
123 × 82 cm
Kunsthaus, Zürich

Although caught *en face* and half-length, this female figure is not the type to lower her eyes when someone is looking at her. The frills of her dress, the boa, the left hand resting on her hip in an habitual pose – all of these signs point to her profession. Lautrec painted the blue dress quickly in broad sketchy strokes applied with extraordinary bravura and, as was his custom, concentrated most of his attention on the woman's face. The result was a daring portrait in which the sharp, slightly sidelong look in the eyes returns the indiscreet gaze of the viewer, as if asking: 'Who are you to judge me?' The presence of the whole concealed body is concentrated in the ambiguous smile which wavers between invitation and disdain, in the dominating smile inscribed in the centre of the brightly painted face – transformed into a poisonous bouquet by the ochre and pink make-up with blue reflections.

In 1902, this was the first painting by Lautrec to enter a national collection. It was given by his mother to the Musée du Luxembourg (the collection of works by modern French artists situated in the Luxembourg Gardens on the Paris Left Bank), which accepted it and placed it in the room containing the Caillebotte collection of Impressionist paintings. The painting's entry into the museum followed the rejection of *The Toilette* (page 73) by its steering committee, because the work's subject was considered too indecent.

Woman with a Black Boa

Painted 1892
52 × 41 cm
Musée d'Orsay, Paris

As he often did, for this composition Lautrec used his friends and acquaintances as models: on the left, in a top hat, we find François Gauzi, at the far right the painter Charles Conder, while the woman moving away and seen from the back is Jane Avril. The dancer in a black hat is Cha-U-Kao. Nevertheless, this painting is certainly not a juxtaposition of portraits.

The foreground and middle ground are related primarily through the use of colour – the particular shade of dark blue speckled with mauve which passes from one garment to another and in contrast to which the red of the blouse strikes a particularly strident note. At the same time the background, which is treated in much lighter shades, defines the architectural space in a vague manner. Despite this, the characters are represented in different ambiences which do not communicate with each other. From this point of view, Jane Avril is isolated in an enigmatic solitude in relation to the figures who are shown as couples in paired groups. The two dancers also appear enclosed in their own universe: the one on the left is the only smiling character, while in their portraits, in the way in which Lautrec painted the details of their gestures and their hands in order to suggest the true friendship between them, we can make out signs of tenderness and even of complicity without any voyeurism. In this space, where people's lives merely cross each other, the two dancers at least share their waltz, and probably more – even though Cha-U-Kao, instead of responding to her partner's look, keeps her eyes closed.

At the Moulin Rouge: Two Women Dancing

Painted 1892
95 × 80 cm
Narodnì Gallery, Prague

This lithograph was preceded by an oil painting in which La Goulue's silhouette was accentuated in a kind of pictorial gesture which attempts to capture a fugitive motif at the same time as conferring upon it a meaning which transcends the anecdotal circumstance from which it arose.

The slanted balcony, on which a number of revellers are enjoying themselves, creates in this modestly sized cartoon a perspective which is not only spatial but also chronological. The massive silhouette of the sister, Jeanne Weber, also known as Môme Fromage ('Cheese Girl'), prefigures what La Goulue's is to become: she holds her destiny by the arm. Jeanne had appeared alongside her famous sister in an earlier oil painting, *La Goulue at the Moulin Rouge*, in which her vast figure was halved lengthwise by the frame.

In the lithographic interpretation of this scene, completed during the same year, Lautrec used flat tints which systematize the contrast between the pink (of La Goulue's dress) and the black (of her sister, and of other characters). Thus, symbolically, the seductive appeal of a body whose mobility is stressed by the gesture of the hand holding the waist is trapped by masses of dark colour. She still reigns, in her braggart way, but only because of her fragile and unusual youth: the black scarf in the shape of a dog-collar on her neck announces the future victory of time, which will one day transform her into what her sister already is.

La Goulue and her Sister at the Moulin Rouge

Printed 1892
46.1 × 34.8 cm
Musée Toulouse-Lautrec, Albi

100

In its original conception, this was a much smaller painting and, as is obvious to the naked eye, the bottom and the right borders have been added on to the smaller central scene. There is contradictory evidence as to the chronology of the enlargement and some question as to whether the central scene was painted before or after the addition of the two strips of canvas. Whereas Joyant dated the central scene as having been painted in 1892 and the addition – with the female figure on the right representing May Milton – made in 1895, recent research has shown that the whole image was painted at the same time and the margins removed possibly some time after Lautrec's death, as is clear from the photographic reproduction of the painting without the marginal strips in the April 1902 issue of *Figaro illustré*. It is also possible that Lautrec changed his mind and, as he did with some other proejcts, enlarged the canvas himself before painting it and turned it into a large-scale composition comparable in size and scope with the 1889–90 *Dance at the Moulin Rouge* (page 75).

The characters belong to the familiar world of Lautrec's friends and cabaret performers. The sitting figures can be easily identified as the critic Edouard Dujardin, the Spanish dancer La Macarona, Paul Sescau and Maurice Guibert. La Goulue is adjusting her hair in the background and Gabriel Tapié de Céleyran, accompanied by Lautrec himself, is caught walking across the dance stage without interacting with any of the other characters. The face of the female figure on the right, strangely lit from below, contrasts with the calm disposition of the seated group.

The multiple activities of these four groups – the seated party, Lautrec and Gabriel, La Goulue and her companion, and the woman in the foreground, making four areas between which there is no communication – stress their isolation and solitude. As a place of convergence and dispersion, the Moulin Rouge welcomes heterogeneity, just like the painting which combines portraits and caricature, the visible and its

At the Moulin Rouge

Painted 1892
123 × 141 cm
The Art Institute of Chicago

_____

interpretation, shapes and colours, agreement and dissonance, the awakened state and the nightmare.

By putting the figures in close-up and cutting some of them off by the frame, Lautrec places the spectator in the scene which he portrays. This oil painting is sometimes also called *The Interior of a Cabaret* or *L'Assommoir*, a title which seems to suit its ambience better: in the faces and silhouettes there are no traces of joy or pleasure, nothing to evoke the atmosphere of a dance. Every character is fixed in isolation, which seems irrevocable, and the looks of each of them are directed towards different spectacles and objects. By using a very rich chromatic range Lautrec did not contradict the impression of sadness and depression which this painting produces. On the contrary, the wealth of colours only gives a richer version of it: beyond the coloured appearance is the triumph of a uniform gloom. This is one of the rare paintings which justify a comparison between Lautrec's work and the writings of contemporary Realist or Naturalist authors such as Octave Mirbeau or J.-K. Huysmans.

Whereas this particular layout had become possible only after the experiments of the Impressionists, Lautrec's use of it has nothing in common with the theoretical preoccupations of the movement, either in terms of the definition of various planes and independent masses of light, or in terms of psychology.

A Corner of the Moulin de la Galette

Painted 1892
100 × 89 cm
National Gallery of Art, Washington DC

In the numerous portraits and studies of Jane Avril completed in 1892–3, Lautrec always represented her at least apart, if not completely alone, utterly absorbed by her own private universe. In this composition, this singularity and isolation is suggested by the way in which she is obviously dancing for her own pleasure. Nevertheless, if we are to believe Paul Leclercq's testimony, her movements fascinated the public: 'In the middle of the crowd there was shuffling, a living hedge was formed, Jane Avril was dancing, turning gracious, light, slightly crazy, pale, slim, racy ... she turned and turned, weightless, nourished on flowers.' But Lautrec did not care for the success she enjoyed with the regular visitors to the Moulin Rouge; he was interested in stressing her personality, focusing on the precise outlines of her face. Whereas La Goulue belonged entirely to the world in which she developed, Jane Avril was different from it, and therefore attracted even more attention. When Lautrec represents her entering the Moulin Rouge, she is wearing a coat, obviously coming in from the outside, different from La Goulue, who is always shown dressed in her professional outfit (page 93). Here she wears a properly bourgeois blouse which provides a contrast to the frenetic movement of her legs, though this does not make us think that she has become dissolute. She appears to be completely in charge and she alone decides what is suitable for her.

Jane Avril Dancing

Painted 1892
84 × 44 cm
Musée d'Orsay, Paris

Le Divan Japonais, which first opened its doors in 1889, owed its name to its décor (which was actually more Chinese) of lanterns and bamboo chairs and to the costumes worn by the waitresses. It was a popular version of the pervasive fashion for things Japanese, which also included admiration for Hokusai prints, *Madame Chrysanthème* and a work on Utamaro published by Edmond de Goncourt in 1891. In this poster, commissioned by the owner of the *café-concert*, Jehan Sarrazin, Lautrec played with double displacement: of the spectacle towards the spectators – he cut off Yvette Guilbert's head and centred the image on Jane Avril's curvy body – and of the exotic décor towards stylistic appropriation. The shadows of the musical instruments sticking out of the orchestra pit are rendered in such a dynamic fashion that they appear to be alive, and the head of the music critic Edouard Dujardin, with his hair and beard continuing the yellow counterpoint of Jane's chair and his cane, seems more like a theatrical mask. The use of a flat tint fits the artist's taste for decorative elements (such as the feathers on Jane's hat). Faced with 'this female body in black, as if in armour, stressing the sharp pallor of her profile, with bright red lips under a helmet of golden hair', Thadée Natanson claimed in *La Revue Blanche* to have experienced 'an overpowering artistic emotion'.

Le Divan Japonais

Printed 1892–3
80 × 60 cm
Bibliothèque nationale, Paris

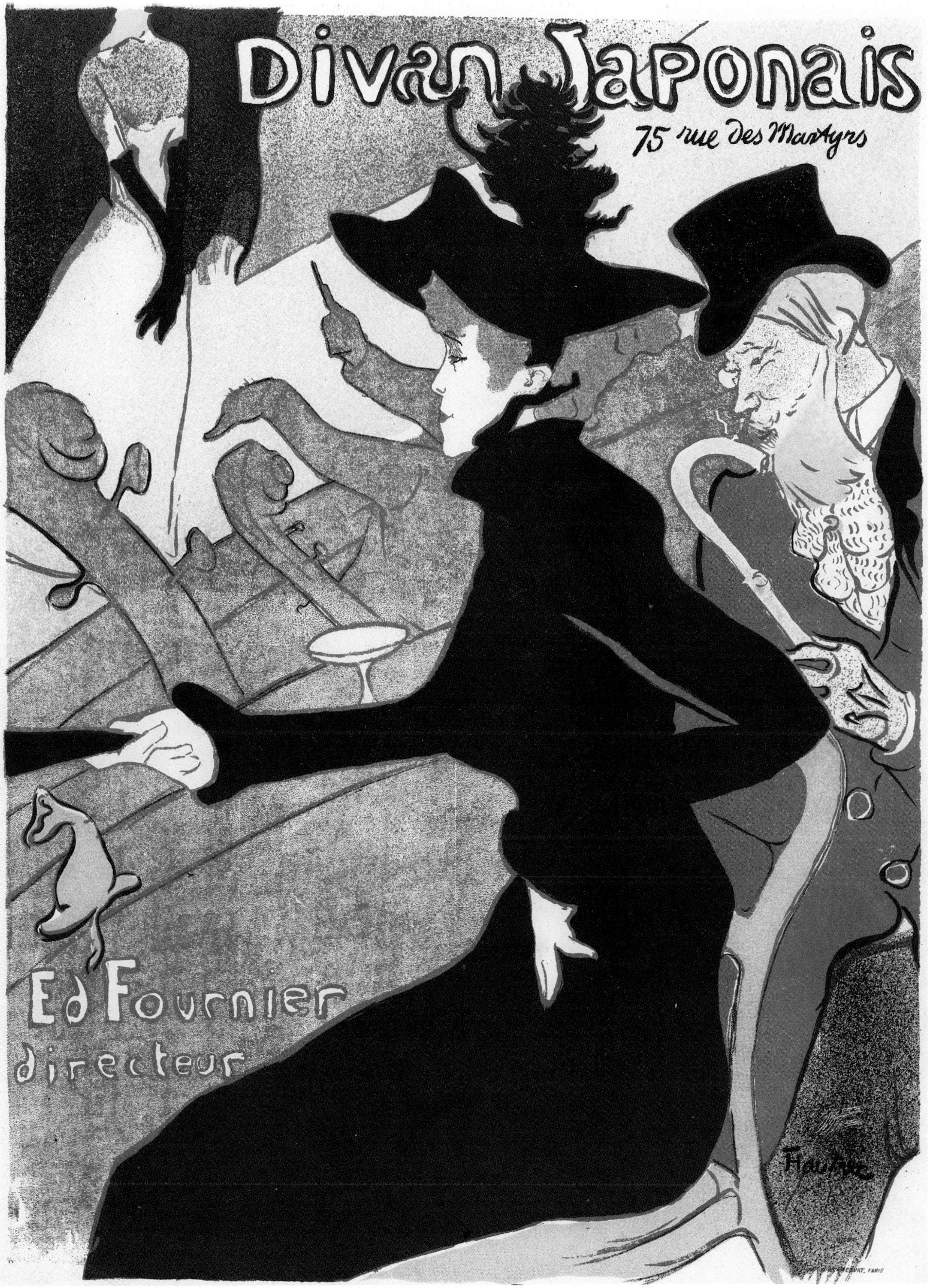
Divan Japonais
75 rue des Martyrs
Ed Fournier
directeur

The Jardin de Paris opened in May 1893 at the rond-point des Champs-Elysées as an elegant extension of the establishments in Montmartre. It soon became a fashionable *café-concert*, but this poster, commissioned at the dancer's request, celebrates the venue by concentrating on its star, Jane Avril (whose name was the only one to appear in the first version). The use of colour was reserved solely for her, as well as the decorative line which prolongs the handle of the double bass and frames the dancer, separating her from the musicians and presenting her as an even more attractive idol because she keeps herself at such a distance. Jane Avril's posture was first studied in a series of sketches on cardboard, then simplified (in the drawing and in the reduction to two colours) through the flattening of the lithographic process: with her left foot placed parallel to the floorboards, she seems to be moving towards the back of the stage, while the neck of the double bass suggests an almost obscene relationship with her raised ankle.

Lautrec's Japanese influences, most visible in the truncated profile and the curly head of the musician, determine decorative effects – the curvy lines, the framing of the image by one of its elements – which were later to be abused by the Modern Style, whereas Lautrec managed to keep a balance by his masterly control of colour.

Jane Avril at the Jardin de Paris
Printed 1893
124 × 92 cm
Bibliothèque nationale, Paris

The American dancer Loïe Fuller, who was simultaneously a singer, musician and tragic actress,
was extremely successful at the Folies Bergère, where
she put on an original performance in which she
moved the long veils of her muslin dress, with the help
of sticks, under the changing colours of the electric
lighting. Disappearing behind the moving shapes
which she created in this way (F. Jourdain thought
that, off stage, she looked like a dumpy school-
teacher with a migraine), she bestowed on the dance a
truly plastic dimension which was obviously intensely
interesting to Lautrec. She was not impressed by his
idea for a poster, so he used his studies for a
fascinating series of lithographs. These were preceded
by an oil study and were published by André Marty in
an edition of about sixty copies. In the lithograph
series Lautrec developed the clear definition of her
veiled appearance by wrapping it in different shades
and by stressing the asymmetry of the veils. Every
plate, hand coloured, offers a different chromatic
scale, thus reinstating the continuity of the spectacle:
spots of golden dust add a reflection which evokes the
play of the light-show.

   Thadée Natanson praised the evocative power of
his friend's lithographs: 'Loïe Fuller closely combines
the flame and the dance. With their metallic glitter,
Lautrec's lithographs capture the reality, or the
apparition, of the living flame, mimicked by flying
veils and by the blaze and shifting colours of the
revolving spotlights.'

Loïe Fuller

Printed 1893
63.2 × 45.3 cm
Musée Toulouse-Lautrec, Albi

Between 1892 and 1895 Lautrec devoted more than fifty paintings to the world of the *maisons closes*. The series reached its peak in this composition, which probably represents the salon of the famous brothel on the rue des Moulins, one of the most luxurious at the time. Having definitively broken away from the kind of painting which could be exhibited at the annual Salon, Lautrec here proposed a very different salon as a substitute.

The orientalizing décor of its interior (arches, columns and leaves) and the dominance of different tones of red (on the floor, the sofas and the walls), combined with the green of the columns and the foliage, create the effect – most likely entirely realistic – of a suffocating greenhouse. The contrasting colours also evoke a garish sort of 'luxury', based on *trompe-l'œil* effects in which the glittering décor conceals its less glossy side.

The made-up faces of the seated women do not smile and their poses appear very rigid: even the figure on the right, with her shirt pulled up, appears immobile. The whole scene, the passivity of the women and the lack of communication between them thus reveals a deadly universe, in which the fake opulence serves merely to cover up its complete emptiness.

This most ambitious of Lautrec's brothel paintings is so lacking in anything aggressive that we now find it hard to believe it could once have shocked the prudery (or hypocrisy) of his contemporaries. Its violence is contained, implicit: the real obscenity lies not in the invitation to carnal love but in its relation to death and decomposition, which is clearly registered in the face of the woman in a long dress, whose body, instead of being naively exposed like those of her colleagues, hides an unknown secret.

In the Salon of the Rue des Moulins

Painted 1894
111 × 132 cm
Musée Toulouse-Lautrec, Albi

Lautrec obviously considered the *Salon* to be one of his more important works. It appeared in the photograph taken in his studio by one of his friends, either Paul Sescau or Maurice Guibert. In this photograph the painting appears already finished and framed, flanked by a naked model holding a spear on the left, with the artist himself standing on the right. Underneath we can recognize three smaller paintings which also feature subjects from the world of prostitution. The staging of this photograph is difficult to interpret, although its self-conscious play on an insider joke is typical of Lautrec.

The artist was cautious of exhibiting the *Salon* publicly and explained his reticence to a friend: 'People might think I wanted to create a scandal.' This was probably one of the works depicting brothel scenes which were hung separately in a room at Joyant's gallery in 1896 to which Lautrec himself kept the key.

In spite of his reluctance to exhibit the painting, he planned to make a colour lithograph of the scene and this pastel version was made for that purpose. Here the architectural details have been simplified, the women's clothing is rendered in a more schematic fashion by means of large surfaces of uniform colour, reminiscent of Lautrec's graphic works. These alterations were necessary for the transfer of the painting on to a lithographic stone. The print was never produced and when Lautrec again took up prints of brothel scenes, they concerned more intimate episodes, *Woman at the Tub* (page 127), for instance.

In the Salon of the Rue des Moulins

Drawn 1894
111 × 132 cm
Musée Toulouse-Lautrec, Albi

This is a project for a poster which was, in the end, rejected by the singer, as a result of the advice of her mother and above all of the writer Jean Lorain, who hated Lautrec. Every one of its features affirms its greatest artistic effectiveness. The singer's silhouette is divided into two sections: the black gloves with their expressive agility, and the face underlined by the black knots holding the dress, with her long neck, her little cherry-shaped mouth, pointed nose, heavily made-up eyes and tufts of thin hair. Having found this effigy too caricatural, Yvette Guilbert wrote to Lautrec: 'For heaven's sake, don't make me so awfully ugly! Just a little less! . . . So many people who have come to visit me screamed in horror when they saw the coloured project . . . Not everyone can appreciate its artistic side . . . '

Her mistake was to forget that, at least in the long term, it is precisely this 'artistic side' which is remembered. Her unique contribution to the history of the *chanson* is much better conveyed in this single painting – with its 'pointed' and ruffled side – than in all the numerous posters which she herself commissioned from other artists, whom we can today reproach for having softened her singular personality precisely in order to make her more appealing.

Yvette Guilbert

Drawn 1894
186 × 93 cm
Musée Toulouse-Lautrec, Albi

Lautrec's cousin Gabriel, the accomplice of many a night spent in theatres, dances and *cafés-concerts*, is here represented without the usual ironic edge, apparent in many compositions in which he appears at the artist's side (page 95) and in which Lautrec takes advantage of the difference in their height for comic purposes. His silhouette, slightly stooping, is distanced from a group of people and his lowered eyes convey neither curiosity nor excitement. The walls create a complex geometrical background and the open door of a box reveals a corner of the stage curtain. The red carpet, rendered in broad, curving brushstrokes, indicates the slight bend of the corridor of the Comédie Française. Its audacious colour contrasts with Gabriel's black silhouette and the dark green dresses of the figures in the background, whose caricatured faces have been compared with those of Goya and Ensor.

Lautrec took pleasure in making fun of his cousin and was often rude to him, especially as Gabriel seemed sincerely to appreciate the painter's talent – he helped Joyant to gather paintings for the Lautrec collection in the museum in Albi, which was completed in 1922. This portrait reveals the deep friendship which united the two men and in its own way symbolizes the artist's debt: since Gabriel was able to put up with Lautrec in spite of everything, he was compensated at least with a painting of himself from which he could get some satisfaction.

Dr Tapié de Céleyran in a Theatre Corridor

Painted 1894
110 × 56 cm
Musée Toulouse-Lautrec, Albi

Unlike the other portraits of her by Lautrec in which she is shown already in her costume, Cha-U-Kao is represented here at the point where she assumes the character in her dressing-room. The reflection of a man in evening dress in the mirror tucked in the upper left-hand corner brings the outside world into this otherwise very private scene. This is a transitional moment between her intimate truth and her social role, captured in such a way that neither of the two sides dominates: the wig is not yet permanently fixed, the enormous yellow collar appears more cumbersome than appealing. Nevertheless, instead of stressing the unintended comic potential of the scene, Lautrec exploits it for lavish chromatic harmonies – between the wall, the muslin, the costume and the couch – and strives to render the grace of the unselfconscious gesture of the woman's arm and her bent neck. His priority is to use the painting as a means not of deriding the characters he represents, but rather of revealing the unsuspected beauty which can be found even in circumstances and places where no one expects it.

The painter's gaze is on the lookout for the unexpected; he is able to seize something which appears or happens only once, by chance, just like the later photographers of everyday life – and Lautrec was aware of the possibilities of photography, even though in his time one had to keep still and pose for a relatively long period. The work of the painter then consists of restoring the unique aspect of that moment, as if it happened only for the spectator.

This is nevertheless the painting which its first owner, the celebrated Paris collector Isaac de Camondo, unable to understand the painter's intentions, hung in a private room – away from the rest of his collection, which was permanently on show.

The Clowness

Painted 1895
57 × 42 cm
Musée d'Orsay, Paris

When the publisher of *La Revue Blanche* asked him to create the new poster for the magazine (the previous year it had been designed by Bonnard), Lautrec decided to use as the basis for his design – apart from the title, information on the frequency of issues and address of the editorial offices – the figure of Misia Natanson. The wife of the journal's editor-in-chief Thadée Natanson, and friend and muse of many contemporary painters, this beautiful, lively and intelligent woman was the perfect emblem for the fashionable and avant-garde style of the magazine. She had been painted frequently by Bonnard and Vuillard and was known to be an excellent pianist.

Lautrec elaborated her silhouette in two preparatory drawings, of which the second is larger than the definitive poster itself. The figure is captured from the side: she is skating but appears reduced to an elegant motionless silhouette. In every detail of her appearance she symbolizes the novelty and the audacity of the publication: the flat hat with the huge ostrich feather (which reminds us of Jane Avril's crest in the poster for the Divan Japonais, page 101), the veil and the short fur jacket all show an elegance without ostentation. On the lithographic poster the lines of perspective disappear, the body leaning slightly forward being enough to evoke energy; the face is reduced to a few features and the red dots on the dress are echoed in the spider-form decorations on the jacket, the muff and in Misia's pouting lips.

Misia Natanson (poster for *La Revue Blanche*)

Printed 1895
130 × 95 cm
Musée Toulouse-Lautrec, Albi

La revue
blanche
bi-mensuelle
le nº 60 cent.
12 francs par An
1 rue Laffitte
Paris
Charpentier et Fasquelle, éditeurs
11, rue de Grenelle

On 6 April 1895, La Goulue, who was no longer performing at the Moulin Rouge – having put on weight, she was performing belly-dances in a fairground stall dressed as an oriental – remembered to call on Lautrec:

My dear friend, I will come to see you on Monday 8 April at two o'clock in the afternoon. My booth will be at the Trône, on the left of the entrance; I have an excellent pitch and would be very happy if you would have time to paint something for me. If you can tell me where to buy the canvases, I will bring them over the same day.

Even though he was already keeping his distance from the Montmartre dance halls and turning to new themes, Lautrec welcomed this opportunity to create two large decorative panels of his own choice, designed to be shown to a general public. The one on the left represents the past, on which the dancer's reputation was based. Famous for her wild *quadrille naturaliste*, La Goulue, and in particular her dress, is composed in quick, broad brushstrokes used by Lautrec for capturing the fleeting scenes of cabaret life. Next to her, the elongated figure of her old partner Valentin seems much closer to a caricature than to a portrait.

In the background, Lautrec has once again placed several of his well-known characters and types: Père Pudeur, the conductor Dufour, several revellers, among them Jane Avril in the company of Maurice Guibert, whose red bow-tie is the only spot of bright colour in the entire painting, and another dancer. The lanterns hanging over the background (and the not so lively dancers) provide the transition to the panel depicting the present. Both panels were placed at the front of the stall, one on either side of the entrance.

Dance at the Moulin Rouge

Painted 1895
298 × 316 cm
Musée d'Orsay, Paris

In this panel La Goulue is represented in profile in her supposedly 'oriental' routine, which is given some authenticity by the other two costumed characters present on the stage and by the crescent moons on the rear panel.

Lautrec took advantage of this opportunity to install, in the foreground, with his usual sense of humour, a group of silhouettes observing the performance and consisting of connoisseurs (if the public were able to recognize them, their names would provide the best guarantee for the quality of the spectacle) such as Tinchant the pianist from Le Chat Noir, the photographer Paul Sescau, the champagne merchant Maurice Guibert, his cousin Gabriel, and the massive figure of Oscar Wilde; we can also recognize the back of Jane Avril, under another one of her extravagantly large hats and, next to her, that of the painter himself; finally, in profile, none other than Félix Fénéon, the art critic of infallible taste.

This alignment of spectators inverts the composition of the poster for the Moulin Rouge (page 79). What, on the poster, was a frieze of shadows here becomes illuminated, but we are not necessarily supposed to think that La Goulue is reduced to being a shadow of her earlier self.

Both panels have lost some of their colour through extremes of weather and it is therefore difficult to decide if Lautrec devoted as much care to their colouring as he did to the choice of characters.

In 1900 La Goulue, whose belly-dancing was no longer popular, sold the panels. One of the subsequent owners, the art dealer Hodebert, cut up the panels into eight sections and several smaller parts in order to sell them more easily and they were only reassembled in 1929, the year of La Goulue's death.

The Moorish Dance

Painted 1895
285 × 307 cm
Musée d'Orsay, Paris

Lautrec had first met Oscar Wilde in Paris, but the famous Irish writer had refused to pose for him. This portrait was executed from memory at the time of Wilde's celebrated trial in London.

As is often the case in Lautrec's portraits, the background is very subdued; its function is merely to suggest a vaguely London-like townscape and under-line the refined shade of the dandy's blue jacket. The painter's attention is here once again concentrated on his model's face: the drawing emphasizes the swollen eyelids, the excessively made-up red lips, and the hefty figure. Nevertheless, this insistence on the writer's worn-out physical appearance does not imply any sort of moral judgement: the painter is merely trans-posing the image Wilde projected of himself – in which disdain is mitigated by weariness and uncon-ventional behaviour by obvious decay. In 1895 Wilde was only thirty-nine and Lautrec showed him as a 'boyish old man', already at the end of his reign and vanquished by the oppressive puritanical mentality from which he claimed to have broken free.

Lautrec used this watercolour the following year as a basis for the design of a programme for a double bill of *Raphaël* by Romain Coolus and Wilde's *Salomé*, commissioned by Lugné-Poé, the actor-manager of the Théâtre de l'Œuvre. *Salomé* was being staged in Paris although it had been banned by the authorities in London and its author had faced prosecution for homosexuality. The figure of the controversial Irish poet appeared once again in Lautrec's design for the advertisement in *La Revue Encyclopédique*.

Oscar Wilde

Drawn 1895
90 × 50 cm
Lester Collection, Beverly Hills

In the summer of 1895, during another voyage on board the *Chili*, Lautrec was captivated by the unusual beauty of a female passenger who often sat on deck either reading or dreamily gazing at the ocean. Though we do not know her name, we do know that she occupied cabin 54 and was said to be married to a civil servant on a posting to Dakar. Lautrec never spoke to her but often made slow, amorous drawings of her silhouette. Once he had reached Bordeaux, his original destination, Lautrec decided to follow her to the end of her voyage. In the end, his travelling companion Maurice Guibert managed to persuade him to leave the ship in Lisbon. Nevertheless, Lautrec asked the captain to send a telegram from Dakar in the artist's name to his friends in Paris.

Upon his return to Paris, Lautrec designed a lithograph, based upon a combination of his memories, sketches he had made during the journey and, most likely, a photograph – taken without the unknown woman's knowledge. Shielded underneath an awning, but in full light, lost in her contemplation of the sea on which a steamer can be made out through the waves, her book having slipped from her hand, this beautiful woman embodies elegance and youth. Every line is drawn with infallible certainty, the soft colours evoking a dream which the dreamer herself is desperate to retain.

In 1896 this lithograph was used as a poster both for the international poster exhibition known as the Salon des Cent, and once again during the same year, for the exhibition organized by the *Libre Esthétique* in Brussels.

The Passenger in Cabin 54

Printed 1896
60 × 40 cm
Bibliothèque nationale, Paris

This is the fifth plate from the collection *Elles* and the most 'modest' in the whole series – if we exclude the portrait of Cha-U-Kao – as it refers the least directly to the world of the *maisons closes*. The drawing of the woman's bent silhouette is given priority, inscribed as it is in a trapezium whose top represents the complex arrangement of her crumbling hairdo. Lautrec elaborated the woman's posture in several preliminary drawings, which testify to his frequent reworking of contours, and also led to the late addition of the corner of the bed, which is visible in the lower right-hand side of the plate.

The scene could represent the completely innocent daily preparations for a toilette; indeed, the fireplace, with a decorative grandfather clock placed on the mantelpiece in bourgeois fashion, and the bed, reflected in the mirror of an ordinary wardrobe, would lead us to suppose exactly that. The only signs which could encourage a different interpretation are the drawing pinned to the wall which depicts Leda and the Swan – a theme with an unlimited potential for erotic exploitation – and the fan slipped behind the frame (although even this could easily be the innocent souvenir from a party).

The soft colours of the grey, pink and yellow themselves give this room an air of enigmatic light, like sunlight passed through a sieve. Lautrec here played with the ambiguity of his title: it is not easy to define or classify this woman. It is therefore preferable to enjoy the skill with which he has indicated the folds of her gown by means of a few masterly movements, which distribute the downstrokes and the upstrokes in thick lines.

The flattened perspective given by the sloping floor and the complementary warm tonalities resemble the technique of Japanese prints, in particular those of Utamaro, which were very fashionable at the time and which influenced so many younger artists.

Woman at the Tub

Printed 1897
52.5 × 40 cm
Bibliothèque nationale, Paris

Lautrec met Paul Leclercq, the young writer, one of the founders of *La Revue Blanche* and its first editor-in-chief (before it was taken over by the Natanson brothers), in 1894. In the little volume of his *Mémoires*, Leclercq described the conditions in which this portrait was painted: having visited the studio in the avenue Frochot for over a month, about three or four times a week, he remembered very clearly that he 'did not actually pose for Lautrec for more than two or three hours in all'. At every session the painter would place his model in a large wicker armchair, look at him through his pince-nez and then apply just 'a few light brushstrokes of highly dilute paint', after which he would quickly declare 'Enough done! It's too hot!' before accompanying his friend for a stroll.

Lautrec's apparent facility as a painter, which this episode demonstrates, not only presupposes an obvious technical mastery, but also suggests his knowledge of a certain number of possible 'models': there is no doubt that, in this case, works by Whistler, whom Lautrec greatly appreciated, had suggested the chromatic relations and their respective values. Nevertheless, Lautrec stayed within his favoured portrait manner, even though this particular painting is quite unusual in its long format. This was possibly because Lautrec was still getting used to his new studio at the moment it was conceived, and the best way to achieve this was to organize it pictorially. Thus the elaborate figure appears detached, against a quickly sketched background on which we can recognize the outlines of the *Passing Conquest*, which seems to be in the middle of being painted, although it was certainly finished by 1897. The presence of an earlier work indicates an intellectual complicity between the two men which cannot be explained away in terms of a simple portrait commission.

Portrait of Paul Leclercq

Painted 1897
54 × 64 cm
Musée d'Orsay, Paris

It was again while passing through Le Havre on the way to Bordeaux (page 125) in July 1899 that Lautrec was captivated in The Star, a small *café-concert* popular among the sailors, by the beautiful face of the local barmaid, who probably also sang at times. As there was intense boat traffic in the English Channel, the port offered a number of *cafés-concerts* and bars which catered for British sailors and which were staffed with British performers.

Having been released, as he himself described it later, 'out of gaol', Lautrec rediscovered the freshness of a face underlined by the silky texture of an elegant neck topped by hair composed in skilfully arranged curls, just as he liked them. He made several drawings of the sitter, as he mentioned in a letter to Joyant, asking his friend to send him some painting materials. He stayed several days at the Hôtel de l'Amirauté in La Havre, where he finished this portrait on a panel before sending it to Paris with a request that it should be framed without delay.

The artist obviously regarded the work as doubly successful, both as a painting and therefore as a sign of his return to normal life. While this bust-length portrait of a woman with a pert expression and fresh complexion is particularly charming – with its smile, dimpled cheeks and its delicate colouration – its background is all the more surprising. It consists of a network of lines, as if taken from fantastic architecture, and spots that correspond to each other in a screen where the blue, green and pink provide an echo of the model's dress – as if she had the power to alter the colour of her surroundings to suit her mood.

Miss Dolly – the name given to her by Joyant, who knew the circumstances behind the origin of this painting very well – reappeared in a lithograph completed later that autumn in Lautrec's studio in Paris.

The English Girl at The Star in Le Havre

Painted 1899
41 × 32.8 cm
Musée Toulouse-Lautrec, Albi

From 1898 onwards, the old equestrian themes appeared once again in Lautrec's lithographic output. The following year, the largest number of plates – with the exception of the illustrations he made for Jules Renard's *Histoires naturelles* – was devoted to this subject. *The Jockey* – the first in a series of racing prints in colour, commissioned by the publisher Pierrefort – is distinctive on account of its incontrovertibly successful artistry. This was, apparently, an entirely traditional motif and so was the way in which the artist approached it; however, Lautrec showed himself able to convey an unusual dynamism, and the impression of both power and speed, through his particular layout. Two mounts racing towards the winning-post make the two jockeys, whose faces are concealed, seem like natural excrescences of their shapes. Lautrec was interested in representing the unity of the horse and its rider, the encounter of muscle and will joined together in a shared aim. In a foreshortened perspective, the animal in the foreground becomes an almost mythical creature, able to provoke both enthusiasm and passion. The horse by itself suggests the ambience of a racecourse: it does not have to touch the ground, and the nervousness of the drawing gives to its elongated head an unreal appearance. This impression is reinforced by the predominance of dark tones, in a contrast with the neck, which is large and more clearly defined, representing the true concentration of energy.

The absence of strong shades turns this spectacle into a dream-like vision – unless this is a modernized and partial version of the Riders of the Apocalypse.

The Jockey

Printed 1899
52 × 37 cm
Bibliothèque nationale, Paris

In May 1900 Lautrec and his faithful 'keeper' Paul Viaud spent some time in Crotoy, where Maurice Joyant later joined them. Lautrec took advantage of this visit and added to the series of portraits of his friends and relations – which had made up a large proportion of his work since he had left the clinic – with an image of Joyant dressed and equipped for duck-hunting, standing on the bridge of a ship. This oil painting on wood, produced following a painted study and a few sketches, was completed rapidly in about ten sessions. From the sitter's testimony we know that Lautrec was physically unable to work for extended periods of time and that these sessions exhausted him.

The speed of painting is apparent in the original pictorial treatment: the broad brushstrokes which define the colour of the oilcloth do not cover the surface completely and leave the texture of the base visible. The surrounding landscape is treated even more casually than in the earlier portraits which the artist had painted in the open air. The brown glaze is enough to evoke the seaside atmosphere in its autumnal tones rather than those typical of springtime. The slightly bent posture and the hands firmly holding the gun confer on Joyant an air of fierce determination, stressed also by his strong profile.

The placing of the figure in the centre of the panel transforms a holiday memory into an allegory of the hunt, though admittedly not a very serious one.

Maurice Joyant at the Baie de Somme

Painted 1900
116 × 81 cm
Musée Toulouse-Lautrec, Albi

The painter's last completed female portrait was of 'a young milliner with sumptuous blonde hair and the fine face of a lively squirrel whom [Lautrec] called Croquezy-Margouin or just Margouin'. As Paul Leclercq described, 'In her company, Lautrec behaved like a child with another child.' There were good reasons for this: Louise Blouet, employed at a hat shop as a model and seamstress, was in fact the mistress of one of the artist's friends. The nickname Lautrec had bestowed on her consists of a word of advice, 'Croquez-y' (which could mean both 'Sketch her' and 'Taste her'), together with the slang name for the female mannequin in a fashion shop.

She was Lautrec's last passion and appeared in many of the drawings, pictures and lithographs which he completed that year. This beautiful young woman with regular features and remarkable hair is portrayed sitting in her hat shop, and the motif of her hairstyle is repeated in the elegant hats which surround her. She is made even more desirable by her modestly lowered eyelids, which apparently do not see the desire she provokes. This desire envelops the painting, turning the model's blouse into a theatre of shades and caressing brushstrokes, and it gives a bluey-green atmosphere to the hat shop as a whole.

In *The Milliner* Lautrec makes the feminine sacred and represents for the first time a woman as attractive, but at the same time forbidden. She is fascinating, but like a trap: full of light, but enclosed by shade. The flamboyant hair reminds us of a setting sun: in this final portrait manages once again to go through that kind of alchemy which transforms a dream of possession into the reality of a painting.

The Milliner

Painted 1900
61 × 49.3 cm
Musée Toulouse-Lautrec, Albi

This composition, the last significant painting by the artist, was undertaken to commemorate Gabriel Tapié de Céleyran's defence of his doctoral thesis, which had occurred two years previously. Lautrec found in this theme a pair of suitable emotional elements: his cousin and devoted friend Gabriel, and the medical milieu, which he had not painted for almost ten years. This time he represents neither people celebrating nor characters weighed down by boredom, but a serious and dignified event.

The upper part of the canvas is cut off horizontally by a large window, the only source of light. Using an even more sombre palette than for the series inspired by *Messaline*, Lautrec, who had made his reputation with clear and attractive shades, encountered new problems, such as the reflection of light on a forehead and the glow of red in a setting of dark shades. We can discern here an anticipation of Rouault, but also a recollection of the work of Forain or of Daumier.

This painting has often been the object of negative criticism and has been described as 'clumsily handled' and as showing signs of the painter's fatigue. There is not a trace of irony in the portraits, but in the foreground the hands and arms of the characters are abnormally developed. Is this a result of a serious error in the drawing or is it an intentional distortion made with the expressive power of the scene in mind? It is difficult to resolve this enigma because of the lack of other canvases in the same vein.

Is it possible that, having exploited all the possibilities of drawing, Lautrec had decided to have as his main priority in this work the development of his handling of colour? This attractive hypothesis, which would indicate a choice of a new style, or maybe even of a new career for the painter, cannot be verified, and the last works keep their secret, offering themselves up to contradictory interpretations, according to whether we deplore the decline of the draughtsman or admire the artist as a colourist of unusual skill.

An Examination at the Faculty of Medicine, Paris

Painted 1901
65 × 81 cm
Musée Toulouse-Lautrec, Albi

NOTES

1 Quoted in P.H. Huisman and M.G. Dortu, *Lautrec by Lautrec*, p. 31.

2 That is, almost a tenth of his complete output of paintings, though they were rough sketches in small formats.

3 Quoted in *Lautrec by Lautrec*.

4 J. Meriem, 1882; quoted in the catalogue *Equivoques*, Musée des Arts décoratifs, Paris, 1973.

5 G. Lafenestre, 1888; quoted in *Equivoques*.

6 In 1905, as President of the Museum Council, Bonnat was against putting Lautrec's paintings in the musée du Luxembourg.

7 Henri de Toulouse-Lautrec, *Lettres 1871–1901*, Paris, 1973, p. 88.

8 Toulouse-Lautrec, *Lettres*, p. 101.

9 Toulouse-Lautrec, *Lettres*, p. 103.

10 In 1896 he declared to Joyant: 'Only the figure exists! Landscape painters are brutes! . . . Corot, Millet, Manet and Renoir are great because of their figures. What wonders would Monet have achieved had he not been stupid enough to give up the figure?'

11 On this aspect, see Alexa Celebonovic, *The Triumph of Bourgeois Realism*, London, 1974.

12 He repeated the existence in 1889 under the same pseudonym ('Rue Yblas, under the third gas meter on the left, student of Pubis de Cheval, specialist in family portraits with pastel yellow background', specified the catalogue) with a *Portrait of an Unhappy Family Attacked by the Pox*, in the pointillist style. Cf. Catherine Charpin, *Les Arts incohérents (1882–1893)*, Paris, Syros Alternative, 1990.

13 Toulouse-Lautrec, *Lettres*, p. 183.

14 It was the gallery Le Parc de Boutteville, which exhibited works by 'Impressionist and Symbolist painters'.

15 Toulouse-Lautrec, *Lettres*, p. 158.

16 In *La Lithographie*, Paris, 1895.

17 Ernest Maindron, *Les Affiches illustrées*, Paris, 1896.

18 In spite of this, in 1895, three years after the poster for Bruant, the scene curtain at the Ambassadeurs was covered in Chéret's posters: for Saxoléine, the Quincuina Dubonnet, the pastilles Géraudel and Yvette Guilbert.

19 Cf. the study by R. Bargiel and A.M. Sauvage in the catalogue *Toulouse-Lautrec affichiste*, Chaumont, 1990.

20 *The Walk. La Goulue and Jane Avril in the background* (the scene was situated in the Promenade at the Moulin Rouge). The painting belonged to the Josse Bernheim Collection, but it disappeared during the war, having been taken away by the Germans.

21 Nor did he seek *succès de scandale*: at the exhibition of his works in Joyant's gallery, those depicting brothel scenes were hung separately in two rooms on the first floor. Lautrec kept the keys and showed the works only to those he considered suitable.

22 Cf. Yvette Guilbert, *La Chanson de ma vie*, Paris, Grasset, 1927, pp. 224 ff.

23 'I am very busy now with my new job as a set designer; I have to run here and there in order to collect documentation. This is very time-consuming.' *Letters*, p. 209.

24 *Œuvres complètes*, Gallimard, Bibliothèque de la Pléiade, vol. I, pp. 103, 561.

25 'Lautrec certainly has a hell of a cheek, . . . there is no affectation either in his drawing or in his colour. White, black and red in big slabs and simplified shapes – that is his trademark.'

26 Once he borrowed the gig of his neighbour Mallarmé – his old English teacher from the Lycée Fontanès – and returned it after having ironically decorated the sail with his crowned initials.

27 Contrary to some reports, Lautrec did not stop designing posters after Yvette Guilbert refused his project in 1894–5. He made fourteen before 1894, five in 1895, and twelve in the period 1896–9. On the other hand, we can say that, with the exception of *The Passenger in Cabin 54* (see page 125), he showed less inventiveness both in his layouts and in his use of colour. From 1896 on, his creations were not as distinguishable from those of his colleagues as they had been.

28 It seems that he left behind eighty-seven paintings in his old place, with complete indifference.

29 In *La Peinture, suivi de Parlons Peinture*, Denoël, 1950, pp. 404–5.

30 'I am very satisfied [in English in the original]; I believe that you will be even more satisfied,' he affirmed in a note to Joyant when he sent him the paintings.

CHRONOLOGY

1864
24 November – born Henri Marie Raymond de Toulouse-Lautrec-Montfa, in the family mansion Du Bosc in Albi.

1868
Amicable separation of his parents. Starts riding; his education is organized by his family.

1872
The family moves to Paris. Henri enters the Lycée Fontanes, at first obtaining good grades, but does not concentrate on studying. Friendships with his cousin Louis Pascal and with Maurice Joyant. Covers the margins of his notebooks with drawings.

1875
January – leaves the Lycée Fontanes for health reasons. Returns to Albi, and later spends some time at Amélie-les-Bains. Begins to study with a private tutor. Travels to Barèges to undergo various treatments supposed to encourage his growth.

1878
May – the first fracture (left leg) in the hôtel du Bosc. Long convalescence spent at Barèges, Amélie-les-Bains and Nice.

1879
August – the second fracture (right leg) in Barèges. His lower limbs now definitively atrophied.

1880
Visits Nice and spends the summer at the Château du Bosc. Draws military scenes.

1881
Fails the baccalaureate examination in Paris.
During the summer illustrates *Cocotte*, a short story by Etienne Devismes, a friend he had met in Barèges.
November – resits and passes the baccalaureate examination in Toulouse, then returns to Paris where Princeteau expresses enthusiasm for his drawings.

1882
After a winter spent in Albi and Céleyran, works with Princeteau in Paris. Meets John Lewis-Brown, and encounters Forain.
Thanks to a recommendation from his friend Henri Rachou, enters Bonnat's studio. When Bonnat closes his studio, Lautrec passes to Cormon's where he joins his colleagues Anquetin, Gauzi, Grenier and Bernard.

1883
A disappointing relationship with Marie Charlet. Goes with Bernard to visit père Tanguy, who shows them his Cézannes.

1884
Moves in with Albert Grenier, 19 bis rue Fontaine, where he meets Degas. Works at Rachou's or in the garden of the photographer Forest.
Paints the parody on Puvis de Chavannes's *The Sacred Grove*.

Collective exhibition in Pau.
Spends time in Montmartre bars and cabarets.

1885
Opening of Bruant's Le Mirliton. Several of Lautrec's paintings are hung there, among them *The Quadrille of the Louis-Treize Chair at the Elysée Montmartre*. First lithograph, *At the Saint-Lazare*, is based on a song by Bruant.

1886
Rents a studio in the rue Tourlaque. Tumultuous relationship with Suzanne Valadon.
Sends drawings to several journals. Participates in the Fifth Salon des Arts Incohérents. At Cormon's, encounters van Gogh, whose portrait he paints the following year.

1887
Rents an apartment with Dr Bourges.
La Goulue and Valentin le Désossé appear in his work.

1888
Sends eleven paintings to the Exposition des XX in Brussels. Earns good reviews, but Ensor does not appreciate his work.

1889
Exhibits at the Cercle Artistique et Littéraire Volnay and again at the Arts Incohérents.
Spends the summer at Arcachon.
October – *The Dance at the Moulin de la Galette* is shown at the Arts Indépendants.
The Moulin Rouge opens and *At the Cirque Fernando: The Ringmaster* is permanently exhibited in the foyer.

1890
Visits Brussels. Exhibits five paintings at the Les XX exhibition and shows two paintings at the Salon des Indépendants.

1891
January – takes part in the Cercle Volney exhibition. Moves to a new apartment at 21 rue Fontaine. Exhibits ten works at the seventh Salon des Indépendants.
Gabriel Tapié de Céleyran arrives in Paris to study medicine.
Success of the poster for the Moulin Rouge.

1892
Attends the opening of the Cercle Volney exhibition.
February – visits Brussels and exhibits nine works at Les XX. Takes part in the eighth Salon des Indépendants.
May-June – visits London.
Designs the poster for Aristide Bruant, and is asked by Yvette Guilbert to make a poster for her.

1893
January – Dr Bourges marries. Lautrec starts eating regularly at his mother's.
Completes the poster for Le Divan Japonais.
Takes part in the last exhibition of Les XX in Brussels. Exhibits four paintings at the ninth Salon des Indépendants.

Appearance of his poster for Jane Avril at the Jardin de Paris.
First one-man exhibition at the Goupil Gallery.
1894
Visits Brussels (exhibits at the Libre Esthétique show) and London.
Publication of the album on Yvette Guilbert.
Visits Burgos, Madrid and Toledo in Spain.
1895
Completes the decorative panels for La Goulue's dressing-room.
Visits London, and frequents bars near the Opéra.
A liaison with the singer May Belfort.
Boat trip to Lisbon inspires *The Passenger in Cabin 54*.
1896
Exhibition at Joyant's gallery. Goes to Brussels for the Third Salon de la Libre Esthétique.
Vacation with the Natansons at Villeneuve-sur-Yonne.
Publication of the lithograph album *Elles* (a commercial failure).
Visits London, San Sebastian, Madrid, Chambord and Amboise.
1897
Moves to a studio in the rue Frochot. Paints very few oils.
Exhibits at the Libre Esthétique and Indépendants.
Suffers delirious attack in the Natansons' country house, worrying his friends by shooting at invisible spiders.
Back in Paris he enjoys going to lesbian bars.
1898
His London exhibition meets with hostile criticism.
September – spends most of his time cooking at the Natansons' villa, where Vuillard paints a portrait of him.
Suffers another fit in Paris.
1899
Suffers a fit in the rue des Moulins, and is interned (with his mother's consent) in a clinic in Neuilly. Draws circus scenes.
May – released. He lives with a 'guardian', Paul Viaud, a distant relation. Stays in Crotoy, Le Havre, Bordeaux and Arcachon.
1900
Begins to drink again. Works very little and painfully. Expresses little enthusiasm for the Universal Exhibition.
June – establishes himself in Bordeaux and paints the series inspired by *Messaline*.
December – suffers from leg paralysis in Malromé.
1901
April – returns to Paris; organizes his studio, signing some of the works and destroying others.
July – his paintings sell at high prices at a public sale.
August – has another attack of paralysis; his mother takes him to Malromé.
9 September – Henri de Toulouse-Lautrec dies aged thirty-seven.

LIST OF PLATES

All works are by Toulouse-Lautrec unless otherwise identified.

6 *Young Routy at Céleyran*, c.1883. Oil on canvas, 61 × 49 cm. Musée Toulouse-Lautrec, Albi. Photo: Bridgeman Art Library.

9 *Count Alphonse de Toulouse-Lautrec driving his mail-coach*, 1880. Oil on canvas, 38.5 × 51 cm. Musée du Petit Palace, Paris. Photo: Giraudon.

10 Photograph of Lautrec dressed as a choir boy, with Anquetin and Grenier, 1880. Musée Toulouse-Lautrec, Albi. Photo: © Collection Viollet.

13 Photograph of the cabaret entertainer, Artistide Bruant. Photo: © Harlingue-Viollet.

14 *Hangover* (detail), c.1877–8. Black and blue crayon, brush and black ink on paper, 49.3 × 63.2 cm. Musée Toulouse-Lautrec, Albi. Photo: Lauros-Giraudon.

16 *Artilleryman and Woman*, c.1886. Oil on tracing paper, 56 × 45 cm. Musée Toulouse-Lautrec, Albi. Photo: Lauros-Giraudon.

17 *Self-caricature*, c.1895. Musée Toulouse-Lautrec, Albi. Photo: Lauros-Giraudon.

18 *Vincent van Gogh*, 1887. Pastel on cardboard, 54 × 45 cm. Foundation Vincent van Gogh, Vincent van Gogh Museum, Amsterdam.

21 Photograph of the Moulin Rouge with posters by Lautrec, c.1900. Photo © Collection Viollet.

23 Study for *The Moulin Rouge – La Goulue*, 1891. Charcoal, stump, pastel, wash and oil on stained paper, 154 × 118 cm. Musée Toulouse-Lautrec, Albi.

24 Photograph of Toulouse-Lautrec, c.1892. Photo: Viollet.

25 *May Belfort*, 1895. Lithograph poster, 78.8 × 60 cm. Victoria and Albert Museum, London. Photo: Bridgeman Art Library.

27 *Dr Péan Operating*, 1891–2. Peinture à l'essence on cardboard, 73.9 × 49.9 cm. Sterling and Francine Clark Art Institute, Williamstown, Massachusetts.

29 *A Woman Lying in Bed*, c.1896. Pencil and wash on laid paper, 29.2 × 47.5 cm. Courtauld Institute Galleries, London.

30 *Yvette Guilbert Singing 'Linger, Longer, Loo'*, 1894. Peinture à l'essence on cardboard, 57 × 42 cm. Pushkin State Museum of Fine Arts, Moscow. Photo: Bridgeman Art Library.

33 Programme for *The Little Clay Cart*, 1895. Chalk lithograph with spatter, 43.8 × 27.8 cm. Bibliothèque nationale, département des estampes et de la photographie, Paris.

34 *Reine de Joie*, 1892. Lithograph poster with brush and spatter, 149.5 × 99 cm. Private Collection. Photo: Bridgeman Art Library.

36 *Marcelle Lender*, 1895. Bust-length lithograph portrait in six colours, 32.5 × 24.6 cm. Victoria and Albert Museum, London. Photo: Bridgeman Art Library.

38 *Coqs*, 1899. Lithograph illustration for *Histoires Naturelles* by Jules Renard. Josefowitz Collection.

39 *At the Circus – Performing Horse and Monkey*, 1899. Black chalk, coloured crayons and graphite, 44 × 26.7 cm. Private Collection. Photo: Bridgeman Art Library.

41 *Invitation to an Exhibition*, 1898. Lithograph. Musée Toulouse-Lautrec, Albi. Photo: Lauros-Giraudon.

42 Portrait of Henri de Toulouse-Lautrec, after Coquiot, *c.*1896. Photo: © Collection Viollet.

45 *Self-Portrait*, 1880. Oil on canvas, 40.5 × 32.5 cm. Musée Toulouse-Lautrec, Albi.

47 *A Dog-Cart*, 1880. Oil on wood, 27 × 35 cm. Musée Toulouse-Lautrec, Albi.

49 *Study of a Nude*, 1882. Oil on canvas, 55 × 46 cm. Musée Toulouse-Lautrec, Albi.

51 *The Painter, Rachou*, 1882. Oil on canvas, 50 × 61 cm. Private Collection.

53 *Carmen, The Red-Head*, 1885. 23.9 × 15 cm. Musée Toulouse-Lautrec, Albi.

55 *In the Studio. The Model's Pose*, *c.*1885. Oil on canvas, 140 × 55 cm. Musée des Beaux-Arts, Lille.

57 *Portrait of Emile Bernard*, 1885. Oil on canvas, 54.5 × 43.5 cm. Tate Gallery, London.

59 *The Countess Adèle de Toulouse-Lautrec in the Drawing-Room at Malromé*, 1887. Oil on canvas, 59 × 54 cm. Musée Toulouse-Lautrec, Albi.

61 *At the Moulin de la Galette. La Goulue and Valentin le Désossé*, 1887. Oil on cardboard, 52 × 39.2 cm. Musée Toulouse-Lautrec, Albi.

63 *Madame Alice Gibert*, 1887. Oil on canvas, 61 × 50 cm. Private Collection.

65 *At the Bar*, 1877. Oil on canvas, 55 × 42 cm. Mellon Collection, Upperville, Virginia.

67 *Hélène Vary*, 1888. Oil on cardboard, 54.8 × 29.5 cm. Musée Toulouse-Lautrec, Albi.

69 *First Communion Day*, 1888. Oil on cardboard, 61 × 36 cm. Musée des Augustins, Toulouse.

71 *At the Cirque Fernando: The Ringmaster*, 1888. Oil on canvas, 98 × 61 cm. The Art Institute of Chicago. The Joseph Winterbotham Collection.

73 *The Toilette (Red-Head)*, 1889. Oil on cardboard, 67 × 54 cm. Musée d'Orsay, Paris. Photo: © RMN.

75 *Dance at the Moulin Rouge*, 1890. Oil on canvas, 115 × 150 cm. Philadelphia Museum of Art: The H P McIlhenny Collection in Memory of Frances P McIlhenny.

77 *The Streetwalker, or Casque d'Or*, 1891. Oil on cardboard, 64.7 × 53 cm. Philadelphia Museum of Art: The Walter Annenberg Collection.

79 *The Moulin Rouge – La Goulue*, 1891. Lithograph with wash and pastel, 170 × 130 cm. Musée Toulouse-Lautrec, Albi.

81 *Désiré Dihau, Bassoonist at the Opéra*, 1891. Oil on wood, 35 × 27 cm. Musée Toulouse-Lautrec, Albi.

83 *Woman Combing Her Hair*, 1891. Oil on cardboard, 43 × 30 cm. Musée d'Orsay, Paris. Photo: © RMN.

85 *Aristide Bruant at Les Ambassadeurs*, 1892. Lithograph poster with brush and pastel, 150 × 100 cm. Bibliothèque nationale, département des estampes et de la photographie, Paris.

87 *The Hanged Man*, 1892. Lithograph, 123 × 82 cm. Kunsthaus, Zurich.

89 *Woman with a Black Boa*, 1892. Oil on cardboard, 52 × 41 cm. Musée d'Orsay, Paris. Photo: © RMN.

91 *At the Moulin Rouge: Two Women Dancing*, 1892. Oil on cardboard, 95 × 80 cm. Narodni Gallery, Prague.

93 *La Goulue and her Sister at the Moulin Rouge*, 1892. Lithograph with brush and spatter, 46.1 × 34.8 cm. Musée Toulouse-Lautrec, Albi.

95 *At the Moulin Rouge*, 1892. Oil on canvas, 123 × 141 cm. The Art Institute of Chicago. The Helen Birch Bartlett Memorial Collection.

97 *A Corner of the Moulin de la Galette*, 1892. Oil on cardboard, 100 × 89 cm. National Gallery of Art, Washington DC.

99 *Jane Avril Dancing*, 1892. Oil on cardboard, 84 × 44 cm. Musée d'Orsay, Paris. Photo: © RMN.

101 *Le Divan Japonais*, 1892–3. Chalk lithograph with brush and spatter, 80 × 60 cm. Bibliothèque nationale, département des estampes et de la photographie, Paris.

103 *Jane Avril at the Jardin de Paris*, 1893. Lithograph with brush and spatter, 124 × 92 cm. Bibliothèque nationale, département des estampes et de la photographie, Paris.

105 *Loïe Fuller*, 1893. Oil on cardboard, 63.2 × 45.3 cm. Musée Toulouse-Lautrec, Albi.

107 *In the Salon of the Rue des Moulins*, 1894. Pastel on canvas, 111 × 132 cm. Musée Toulouse-Lautrec, Albi.

109 *In the Salon of the Rue des Moulins*, 1894. Oil on canvas, 111 × 132 cm. Musée Toulouse-Lautrec, Albi.

111 *Yvette Guilbert*, 1894. Oil on paper, 186 × 93 cm. Musée Toulouse-Lautrec, Albi.

113 *Dr Tapié de Céleyran in a Theatre Corridor*, 1894. Oil on canvas, 110 × 56 cm. Musée Toulouse-Lautrec, Albi.

115 *The Clowness*, 1895. Oil on cardboard, 57 × 42 cm. Musée d'Orsay, Paris. Photo: © RMN.

117 *Misia Natanson* (poster for *La Revue Blanche*), 1895. Chalk lithograph with brush and spatter, 130 × 95 cm. Musée Toulouse-Lautrec, Albi.

119 *Dance at the Moulin Rouge*, 1895. Oil on canvas, 298 × 316 cm. Musée d'Orsay, Paris. Photo: © RMN.

121 *The Moorish Dance*, 1895. Oil on canvas, 285 × 307 cm. Musée d'Orsay, Paris. Photo: © RMN.

123 *Oscar Wilde*, 1895. Watercolour on cardboard, 90 × 50 cm. Lester Collection, Beverly Hills. Photo: Giraudon.

125 *The Passenger in Cabin 54*, 1896. Chalk lithograph with brush and spatter, 60 × 40 cm. Bibliothèque nationale, département des estampes et de la photographie, Paris.

127 *Woman at the Tub*, 1897. Lithograph with crayon, brush and spatter, 52.5 × 40 cm. Bibliothèque nationale, département des estampes et de la photographie, Paris.

129 *Portrait of Paul Leclercq*, 1897. Oil on cardboard, 54 × 64 cm. Musée d'Orsay. Paris.

131 *The English Girl at The Star in Le Havre*, 1899. Oil on wood, 41 × 32.8 cm. Musée Toulouse-Lautrec, Albi.

133 *The Jockey*, 1899. Lithograph, 52 × 37 cm. Bibliothèque nationale, département des estampes et de la photographie, Paris.

135 *Maurice Joyant at the Baie de Somme*, 1900. Oil on wood, 116 × 81 cm. Musée Toulouse-Lautrec, Albi.

137 *The Milliner*, 1900. Oil on wood, 61 × 49.3 cm. Musée Toulouse-Lautrec, Albi.

139 *An Examination at the Faculty of Medicine, Paris*, 1901. Oil on canvas, 65 × 81 cm. Musée Toulouse-Lautrec, Albi.

SELECT BIBLIOGRAPHY

AVRIL, Jane 'Mes Mémoires', *Paris-Midi*, 7–26 August 1933.
BOURET, Jean *Toulouse-Lautrec*, Paris, 1963.
BRUANT, Aristide *Dans la rue*, Paris, 1889.
DEVOISINS, Jean *L'univers de Toulouse-Lautrec*, Paris, 1980.
DORTU, M.G. *Toulouse-Lautrec et son œuvre*, 6 vols, New York, 1971.
FOUCART, Bruno *Tout l'œuvre peint de Toulouse-Lautrec*, Paris, 1986.
GAUZI, François *Lautrec et son temps*, Paris, 1954.
GUILBERT, Yvette *La Chanson de ma vie*, Paris, 1927.
HUISMAN, P.H., and DORTU, M.G. *Lautrec by Lautrec*, New York, 1964.
JOYANT, Maurice *Henri de Toulouse-Lautrec, 1864–1901*. I. *Peintre*, Paris, 1926; II. *Dessins, estampes, affiches*, Paris, 1927.
LECLERCQ, Paul *Autour de Toulouse-Lautrec*, Paris, 1920 (republished Geneva, 1953).
LUCIE-SMITH, Edward *Toulouse-Lautrec*, Oxford, 1977 (republished 1983).
MACK, Gerstle *Toulouse-Lautrec*, New York, 1938.
MELOT, Michel *Les Femmes de Toulouse-Lautrec*, Paris, 1985.
MURRAY, Gale *Toulouse-Lautrec: The Formative Years, 1878–1891*, Oxford, 1991.
O'CONNOR, Patrick *Nightlife of Paris: The Art of Toulouse-Lautrec*, London, 1991.
SCHIMMEL, Herbert D., ed. *The Letters of Henri de Toulouse-Lautrec*, Oxford, 1991.
SUGANA, G.M. *Tout l'œuvre peint de Toulouse-Lautrec*, Paris, 1986.
TAPIE DE CELEYRAN, Marie *Notre oncle Lautrec*, Geneva, 1956.
THOMSON, Richard *Toulouse-Lautrec*, London, 1977.
TOULOUSE-LAUTREC, Henri de *Lettres 1871–1901*, Paris, 1973.
WITTROCK, Wolfgang *Toulouse-Lautrec: The Complete Prints*, 2 vols, London, 1985.

PRINCIPAL EXHIBITIONS

Toulouse-Lautrec, The Exhibition on the Occasion of the Fiftieth Anniversary of his Death, Orangerie des Tuileries, Paris, 1951.
Centenaire de Toulouse-Lautrec, Albi–Paris, 1964.
Toulouse-Lautrec: paintings, The Art Institute of Chicago, 1979.
Henri de Toulouse-Lautrec, images of the 1890s, Museum of Modern Art, New York, 1985.
Toulouse-Lautrec, Fondation Pierre-Gianadda, Martigny, 1987.
Toulouse-Lautrec, the complete graphic works, Royal Academy, London, 1989.
Toulouse-Lautrec affichiste, Bibliothèque municipale de Chaumont, 1990.
Toulouse-Lautrec, The Hayward Gallery, London, 10 October 1991 – 19 January 1992, and Grand Palais, Paris, 21 February – 1 June 1992.